HOW TO

MAKE THEM

FRIENDS, FAMILY, EVERYONE

GO VEGAN

Paperback edition: 978-1-5136-4245-1

Ebook edition: 978-1-5136-4269-7

Editing by Darcy Werkman

Full cover design by Damonza

Formatting by Damonza

Special discounts for bulk sales are available. Please contact the author.

To my amazing wife, Bianca, who convinced me to go vegan, and my beautiful daughter, Eliana, who has an incredible heart for all animals.

And to every person that continues to fight for a cruelty-free world.

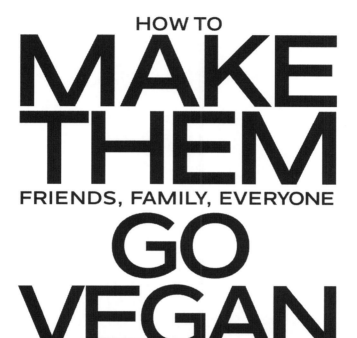

HOW TO
MAKE
THEM
FRIENDS, FAMILY, EVERYONE
GO
VEGAN

ANDREW J PRATT

Foreword by Mic the Vegan

CONTENTS

Special thanks to the following people that contributed to this book:

My wife, Bianca
My sister, Melissa
My friends Rheanna, Kim, Linda, Karissa, and
Mic The Vegan

Everyone that shared their personal stories:

Reign, Andrie, Maayan, Nichelle, Josh,
Cynthia, Nathan, Eugenie, Raluca, Heather,
Jessica, Karen, and Elena

FOREWORD

AJ HITS ON all the familiar myths and illogical notions that keep people from going vegan, like "Cavemen ate meat" and "Plants feel pain." These are cultural memes that are absorbed without a second thought and are not the logically sound reasons for not being vegan that many would like to believe. For example, someone might not go vegan because they think they require animal protein or that, because meat is eaten in nature, it is morally sound. However, some of the simple facts and logic presented in this book can dismantle these myths. All of this is accompanied by the very refreshing fact that AJ has over one hundred references in the back of the book that allow you to trace his points back to their source.

The nuance in the issue here is that effort alone won't accomplish this task because aggressive or misguided attempts to advocate for veganism can backfire. What perhaps sets AJ's writing apart here is that he takes the necessary angle of acknowledging that different types of people—from the "macho" to the environmentalist—must be approached in different ways. All too often, vegans latch on to one-size-fits-all responses that are ineffective and occasionally insensitive. AJ also emphasizes listening, which is perhaps a vegan advocate's most powerful tool because no one wants to be talked at, they want to be talked to.

One thing that adds significant value to AJ's perspective is that he has a background in the armed forces as an Air Force pilot. Often vegans are represented by people like me who, to many folks, come off as "hipster millennials" who don't resonate with much of the population.

However, AJ is a living demonstration of how diverse vegans are—they are all types of people from all walks of life.

At the end of the day, this is a book about people—which is AJ's expertise—and that is the most important topic to focus on. Vegans need to convince others to do the right thing, as much as they would rather just chill with animals instead. Vegans often joke that they like animals better than people because of all the horrible things people do to animals, but I think many people wouldn't want to inflict such harm if they just examined the issue for a moment. I truly believe most people are vegan at heart, and the information in this book can help vegans bring that heart out in others.

—Mic the Vegan
Author and YouTube Personality

INTRODUCTION

So, you want to *Make Them Go Vegan*? Vegan, in my eyes, is anyone that has committed to avoiding the use of animal products or contributing to the exploitation of animals as far as practically possible. I'm going to throw out a wild guess that since you're reading this book, you're already vegan, or close to it. To that, I'd like to say *thank you!* Thank you for convincing yourself that a vegan lifestyle is the best for your health, the planet, and, most importantly, the animals. You are making the world a better place for all of us and your choices have already saved an untold number of lives from slaughter, starvation, and pollution.

That said, if anyone is aware of the challenge to convince someone to go vegan, it should be you; after all, you likely didn't just wake up on day one and say, "That's it, I'm vegan, and that's all there is to it!" No, it probably took weeks, months, or even years to fully commit to changing the habits you've formed over a lifetime. You probably read conflicting information, had friends and family question your choice or try to discourage you, and may have even had a partner that refused to support you. Whatever your barriers were to going vegan, you overcame them all, and if you are like me, it was one of the best decisions you've ever made.

Now that you have become healthier, are aware of the violence in the meat and dairy industries, and see the effects of animal agriculture on the planet, you probably think that you need to convince others to also go vegan. You're not alone! Just about any vegan you talk to has the same desire to help others make the connection and experience all the amazing life changes that come with living compassionately. So how do you do that? Do you go on social media and start sharing videos of abused animals and post "Meat is Murder" on all of your friends' pages? Do you jump your coworkers on the way to the fridge and tell them that their meat-filled lunches will give them cancer? Should you tell your partner to pack their bags and get a lawyer unless he or she gives up animal products immediately?

You can probably see where we are going here, and if you have ever really tried to convince someone to go vegan, you know it's not an easy task. It's not that trying to convince someone is ineffective; rather, we as vegans do a terrible job of doing it the right way. Instead of taking the time to find the right approach, we try to do an all-out assault against others, which usually results in an affirmation of the typical stereotype that vegans are judgmental, pushy jerks.

Just like you, your partner, friends, coworkers, and acquaintances have had a lifetime of conditioning built around the consumption of animal products. They know for sure that you need dairy milk for calcium and meat for protein, that leather is a fashionable product, and that global warming is a hoax. Hence, this kind of social conditioning is not something that is usually overcome in a day or two, or maybe ever.

With that, here is my disclaimer to you: you will not be able to convince every person you know or meet to change their lifestyle, nor can you *make* someone do something they don't want to do. This book is titled Make *Them* Go Vegan, not Make *Anybody* Go Vegan, an important distinction. *Them,* refers to people who are willing and want to change. You can only make others do something they *want* to do, and that is the main purpose of this book, to help you plant seeds that grow into the want for change. That said, the good news is that the vast majority of people you know or meet will be influenced by what you have to say, and you don't have to be an amazing story-teller like James Aspey, as witty as Earthling Ed, or a YouTube star like Mic the Vegan to make an impact.

So what is the best way to persuade someone to make that jump from omnivore to vegan? Is there a magical phrase or a secret video you can show them to change their mind? If there is I have never found it, and just saying "Hey, read this" or "Watch these videos" may spark an interest but rarely does it lead a person to make a lasting change. While some become interested in veganism faster than others, the straightforward reality is that it's a long process for most to become ready to make the decision. You will have to make a compelling case for someone to give up the convenience and habits they currently have, to adopt a new and unfamiliar lifestyle. Furthermore, you may convince a friend to go vegan using incredible logic, stunning health statistics, or riveting videos and think you've found the secret, only to attempt to use the same process on a different friend who instead becomes more entrenched that veganism is not for them. This was my experience.

After convincing a friend to ditch meat products, I felt enabled to help my parents to do the same. In convincing my friend, I shared with her a variety of health studies and appealed to her love of animals. Over many months of answering her objections, she eventually became more and more interested, trying new foods like tempeh and seeing the value of becoming vegan. This all worked so well that when I approached my parents, I was confident the outcome would be the same, but months later they became more against veganism than when I started! What happened? Why didn't my parents react the same way as my friend? Well, I didn't realize their objections—that is, their reasons for not going vegan—would be so substantially different. Further, because it was coming from their son, whom they raised and taught life lessons, they already had resistance to the idea before I could even make a case for it. A one-size-fits-all method would not work to convince them to go vegan, nor many others I talked to later on.

So that's the goal of this book, to empower you with not one, but many skills and methods you can use to engage your family, friends, or anyone in a positive, tactful manner. I created basic strategies for you to connect with others on an individual level and make a personal impact that could break through a lifetime of conditioning. I created groups of people with similar characteristics so you can identify what might be the best approach to bring up the subject of veganism, without ever mentioning the word "vegan." I also made a list of responses to common objections so you can provide a compelling answer on the spot and not miss a valuable opportunity to help others make the connection we all have to our health, animal suffering, and the environment.

Besides what to do, I've included lots of what not to do throughout the whole book as well—many of them my hard-learned failures. In *Star Wars: The Last Jedi*, Yoda said, "The greatest teacher, failure is;" and nothing could be truer. Over the past several years, I tried many times to convince others that a vegan lifestyle was the greatest thing on Earth, and while I think that to be true, they certainly did not. So many times I thought I was armed and ready to teach them why being vegan was so amazing, only to have my facts and knowledge outright rejected. Even with double-blind, peer-reviewed studies in hand to prove that what I was saying was fact, the responses rolled in that "Those studies are trash, and you need to quit pushing your veganism on everyone." If you haven't been told that yet, it's a hard pill to swallow. You know that a vegan lifestyle provides so many positive benefits, yet no one is even willing to hear you out. The piece I was missing was allowing them to make their own discoveries, and the best way to do that is to be a friend and a guide, rather than the typical angry vegan.

That said, it's my hope that I can spare you the wasted time and frustration that I have gone through and help you to guide someone from meat-eater to plant-lover more effectively. There is probably no greater impact you can have on the environment, animal liberation, and global health than convincing another person to give up animal products. You can save the animals, the planet, and our future, by using the information in this book to help others make that leap from unapologetic omnivore to compassionate animal activist. Filled with time-tested techniques for handling people, personal stories from those that have succeeded in convincing others, and tactful methods to get others interested in the vegan lifestyle, you will learn how to break the ice without breaking your relationships. Whether your partner is an avid hunter, your mother is on an all-meat, weight-loss diet, or your friend could never live without bacon, I have a strategy you can use to break down the barriers keeping them from making the change. I'm excited to share so much knowledge with you and grateful that you are willing to accept this challenge to *Make Them Go Vegan*!

CHAPTER 1
MY STORY

HI! MY NAME is AJ. I'm a vegan and an animal rights activist. I grew up, for the most part, in Nashville, TN and now live in Florida, after what seems like a lifetime of moves from state to state. While growing up, the standard American diet was my diet; I ate what I would now consider processed garbage. We didn't have a lot of money growing up, so anything name-brand was a treat, especially the junk food. When I moved out of my parents' house and went to college, I realized all that processed junk wasn't necessarily the best thing to eat, and instead began to embrace a new term going around in 2003: organic foods. I started buying a lot of organic products because they were "healthier," and "better" for the environment. I didn't know it at the time, but that small step laid the groundwork for a more significant step later on.

As part of eating organic foods, I ended up trying a couple of new products that I probably never would have picked up otherwise, namely almond milk and soy milk, as many of the organic products were stuffed together in their own little section of the grocery store. With organic milk being ridiculously expensive, it was only natural to take a peek at some of the cheaper alternatives. One of the first things I tried was almond milk, and let me tell you if you are new to plant-milks, the almond milk of today is quite amazing! Back in 2009 it came in a Tetra-Pak and was clear with bits of almond on the bottom of the package.

When I poured it into a small cup, I was pretty put off; I mean, it looked gross. It looked like thick, cloudy water with almond bits. As awful as it seemed, I tried it anyway, and well, it wasn't great, but it wasn't all that bad either. However, it had such a strong taste that you really couldn't put it on a lot of foods. Needless to say, I didn't buy much of it and only really put it on cereal.

I drank soy milk, too, for a while before learning about the estrogen content. As a guy, who wants to drink estrogen, right? So obviously that wasn't going to work out. There was still really only one choice, which was dairy milk, and that made sense because where else was I going to get my calcium? It was a tough decision because, at that time, I remember reading an article online talking about milk being unhealthy and a major talking point was it's intended for a baby cow, not for people. Even though the article made a solid argument, I ended up rationalizing it away since the other choices I had weren't that great either, or so I thought.

These weren't the only times I unknowingly ventured into a plant-based lifestyle. I once tried some soy hot dogs over concern of sodium nitrate in meat products and a veggie burger just out of curiosity, both of which were pretty good. However, why would I eat "fake" stuff when I could get uncured hot dogs without the nitrate? The big takeaway was that I had the opportunity to try many plant-based products, and even though I didn't add many of them to my diet, I began to incorporate them into my world-view of food.

A few years later, to get rid of my $100 cable bill, I ditched my cable company and got this new cool streaming service called Netflix. Netflix was doing well as a DVD rental company, but the streaming service was brand new. While the content was limited compared to today, it was fun to watch, and a lot of the material was not the typical mainstream shows; rather, a lot of it was unheard of movies and documentaries. One documentary that stuck out was called *Forks over Knives*.

As my wife and I sat down to watch this relatively new film, little did I know that it was going to have a significant impact on both our lives. We watched Dr. Colin T Campbell as he talked about *The China Study* and the astounding results linking animal protein directly to cancer.

We also listened to Dr. Esselstyn as he described how heart disease could be reversed by switching to a plant-based diet.[1] It was eye-opening and well-produced. After watching, both my wife and I were absolutely convinced that we needed to change our eating habits, right? Well, half right.

The documentary had a pretty significant impact on my wife, who also used to be vegetarian, but had very little on me. I thought to myself, *Maybe regular animal products aren't all that great, but we eat organic so that's healthy, right?* She, on the other hand, didn't see it that way. In a bold move, she told me that she would no longer eat meat and dairy and that I could either join her or we could eat separate meals. "Are you serious?" I responded. She was serious. Moreover, she made it a point that I know it wasn't just for health but that she felt eating animals was unnecessary and cruel.

At the time I was a pilot in the U.S. Air Force, an avid runner, and considered myself to be a pretty regular guy. I loved animals because I've always had pets, but I also ate lots of meat and thought animal products complimented my "guy" image. I even used to joke that I wanted a zebra rug for my room, and if I ever flew into Africa I would try to go on a hunt to get an authentic one. Some animal lover, right? I drank organic whey shakes every morning for protein and then again after every workout. I would grill animal products almost every night. In short, I was what most vegans would probably consider a guy who would never go vegan.

My wife, however, certainly didn't think that was the case and she instead, continued to advocate for the animals and answer objections that I had. Resistant, I continued to eat as I always had for about a month, with both of us making separate meals. After several attempts to sway her from the choice she had made, I gave up and agreed to the diet change, because making two different meals every day was just too ridiculous. Did you catch that? I became vegan because I was too lazy to cook more than one meal; how's that for a ground-shaking revelation? At first, I made simple changes, swapping milk for those plant-milks I was familiar with from years ago, and switching out hotdogs for soy dogs. Within a short period, I was eating 100 percent plant-based. Just like that, my laziness to cook had saved hundreds of animals, and after a while, I began to enjoy the change more and more. In my mind, I knew my wife was probably right about the unnecessary suffering of the animals. She would say she's always right, and she was about this.

Over the next couple of months, I was introduced to different media that helped me to move from being a plant-based eater to living and promoting a vegan lifestyle. Dr. Michael Gregor's book *How Not To Die* made me realize that animal products, even organic ones, didn't just promote heart disease and cancer, but had a negative effect on overall health as well. On the odd chance you've never read it, I highly recommend picking it up, or my favorite, listening to the audio version; that way you get the full force of Dr. Gregor's unique personality. The studies in the book were hard to deny, and I was grateful later on to meet him and thank him personally for helping me finally move to a whole-foods, plant-based diet.

Not long after reading *How Not To Die,* I finally got the courage to watch *Earthlings*, a documentary I knew about from Facebook groups and articles online. I quite honestly had avoided seeing it because I had heard of the awful footage it contained. *Earthlings* was undoubtedly the straw that broke the camel's back for me, and after seeing it, I made the real connection to animal suffering. Afterward, I was no longer a vegan for health, but entirely and unequivocally *vegan for the animals*. I've never looked back since. If you have never seen *Earthlings*, it's a compelling inside look into the meat, dairy, and fur industries. It's free to watch every day on YouTube. It's certainly not for the faint of heart, but it's a must watch because nothing can truly make you understand why the vegan movement is so important more than watching the absolute suffering and torture farm animals endure, long before they reach the plates of those who eat them. A key point I want to make as well is that I was mentally ready to watch it, and that is an important takeaway, a topic we will discuss later.

From that moment, I can honestly say a lot changed in my world outlook. I, like many others, could now see the suffering and cruelty that I had been a part of and the impact it was having on the environment. I could see how selfish I had been without even really knowing it, putting my own interests above those of other living and breathing animals that I had written off as lesser beings. These are realizations that I think we all have and that make us so compelled to spread the message of veganism with urgency because it affects so many aspects of morality, health, and climate concerns.

Okay, so why the long drawn out story of my vegan journey? There is certainly nothing unique about it nor did something amazing happen that caused me to make the transition. I didn't bump into a famous vegan celebrity who changed my life. I didn't have some personal overnight transformation that suddenly made me quit eating meat and dairy. What I did have was somebody that initiated a small change that had a big impact as I followed my own route of discovery. The number one single source that gets people interested in becoming vegan is hands down being influenced by another person. According to a Vomad study of 726 vegans, 37 percent were influenced by friends and family or a similar personal relationship (Chart 1.1). Thirty-seven percent![2] That doesn't even include other types of personal interactions such as public activism, lectures, or online discussions that bring it closer to 50 percent.

Chart 1.1: What got you Interested in Veganism? [2]

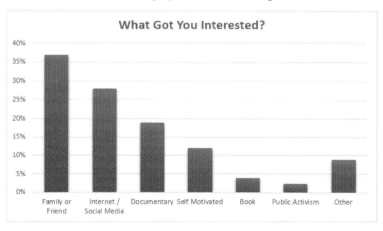

After I went vegan, I had no idea I was a statistic, or that the best way to convince others to go vegan was to engage them personally. All I knew was that I felt compelled to help my friends and family experience the same amazing transformation that I had and see how much of an impact they could genuinely have on the lives of so many animals, on their own health, and on the environment. Even though my full transition had taken over a year, I thought that if my friends and family could watch a couple of the videos I had seen or read the books I had read, they would make the connection faster than I had, and just like that go vegan as well! Of course, I was wrong, and I should have known better.

In my professional life, I make a living by motivating others and instituting change in organizations. A Project Management Professional (PMP) with a Masters of Business Administration (MBA), my career has been dedicated to taking people of all backgrounds and skill sets, making a personal connection, planting the seeds of change and allowing them to grow naturally without the need for confrontation or manipulation. I have to convince others to buy-in to my projects, meet organizational goals, and change processes or culture, and it's often a difficult task. It's a task that comes with many of the same questions people ask when confronted with the choice of going vegan, such as, "I have always done things this way, why would I change?" "What about my objections?" "Why are you trying to change something that isn't broken?" After trying to convince so many people to go vegan with little success, I quickly realized I had been going about it all wrong.

The friends and family I was trying to convince were no different than the people I was working with every day to implement change professionally. They had to be conditioned to accept the change. They needed to have their objections met with clear and compelling answers. Lastly, they had to be motivated and supported to allow the change to happen on their own terms—they had to want the change. So that's what I did; I took my many years of experience and started using the same methodology to begin sowing the seeds of change in my family, friends, coworkers, and everyone I knew. Over time, that one friend I convinced to go vegan turned into two and then many, many more. I now consider myself to be a full-time activist, and regularly engage with as many people as possible to help raise awareness and promote a vegan lifestyle. I plan vegan events in my community like demonstrations and marches,

I fight against animal cruelty in the political arena, I'm an organizer for Anonymous for the Voiceless, a mentor for Challenge 22+, and now my most significant undertaking is becoming a published author.

With that, I'd like to introduce you to this book and the methodology I use to help bring about change in others. In the next chapter, there are some basics that I think are essential to any discussion; things like not trying to argue it out with someone, criticizing others choices, or trying to bombard the other person with facts they have no interest in believing. In Chapter 3, you'll learn how to approach and persuade different types of people in your life—family members in particular. Next, Chapter 4 provides strategies for persuading different categories of friends you might have. Chapter 5 lists responses to common objections, so you will always know what to say when someone puts you on the spot. Finally, Chapter 6 contains lots of stories from others just like you and how they were able to convince their friends and family to make the switch.

In short, this whole book is here for you, to help you, along with my social media pages and website, AndrewJPratt.com, which I keep updated with videos and new information that can help turn the tide in your endeavors to *Make Them Go Vegan*!

CHAPTER 2
THE BASICS

LET'S FACE IT: changing someone's mind is difficult. Cable news spends all day trying to change or affirm our beliefs. Wars are being fought right now because we have differences in opinion on religion, politics, and economics. Even my dogs try to convince me that giving them more treats is the best way to go, and they do an excellent job of it! It seems like everyone is trying to change someone's mind.

So how do you change someone's mind or change their behavior? It might be worthwhile to think about how you changed your own behavior. I'm willing to bet no one threatened you or argued with you till you gave up. You probably heard something that piqued your interest, investigated the information, and decided that making a change was concurrent with your identity and something you wanted to do. That's an important point; you made a change because you wanted to make one and you were willing to listen to the information being presented. This chapter is here to help you to get the other person to lower their natural defenses, so they are more willing to hear what you have to say and are therefore more likely to want to make a change. Things like smiling, matching the other person's tone, and complimenting them go a long way towards making a personal connection and establishing trust.

We will also discuss some common ineffective methods that people typically try to use or worse, use tactics that make others hate vegans.

Things like criticism, arguing with others, or trying to push facts can do just the opposite, creating hardcore anti-vegans that are embittered from endless debates. You probably think I'm joking, but go onto a dairy-friendly Facebook page or Reddit group and let them know you're vegan and watch the fireworks. The people you encounter on there didn't just wake up one day and say I hate vegans; they had lots of experiences with them that formed their opinion that vegans are pushy jerks. Vegans constantly make comments online about how dairy farmers are evil and how people that use animal products are awful, disgusting human beings. You may have even made similar statements online, but on the other side of your screen are people that may have been receptive to a plant-based lifestyle, who are now put-off by vicious comments and argumentative dialogue. I think you'll be surprised by how often people try this forceful method of expressing their views on others, only to end up one or two hours later upset and having accomplished nothing.

No worries, though, because we are going to make sure you don't fall into those same traps that others would have you believe is the way to change minds. As I mentioned before failure is a fantastic teacher, so I'd like to share with you some of my failures—and some successes—that I have seen and experienced. I hope you take them to heart and play the scenarios in your mind as if you were the one on the spot trying to make a case for them to go vegan. By the end, you should have a bag of tips and techniques you can use not only to help others go vegan but anytime you are trying to convince someone to make a change.

CRITICISM

One of the favorite methods of enacting change for people is to criticize others. You don't have to look hard to find examples of it, especially on social media. Speaking of social media, can I be honest? I love Facebook. Not only can I find news faster than just about any other source, but I also have the opportunity to talk to billions of people and share information. I know I don't have to tell you there is also a dark side to Facebook, where people use a variety of off-comments and memes, attempting to win others over to their point of view, usually with little success. If you're a part of any vegan Facebook groups or pages, you may have seen a common method where someone will comment to a non-vegan calling them a "murderer" and let them know that anyone that eats meat is cruel and barbaric. That person then comes back to the vegan group and shares that they "told that person," and everyone celebrates the victory that the vegan message has reached yet another evil meat-eater. It's called criticism, and it happens every day.

So did our activist vegan score one for the home team? Of course not, right? No, all they did was manage to upset some unsuspecting person and criticize their eating habits. That person now likely has a negative view of all vegans, and the next time they talk to or meet another vegan, they will already be preparing to defend their habits or come out on the offensive. Criticism is a sure way never to change anyone's mind and set in place a defense response in that person for the next time they encounter the subject.

For example, take this actual exchange between a vegan activist and a Canadian dairy farm:

Activist: "Some people have empathy and compassion for all animals. Some people don't. These people don't and seem to find pleasure knowing that their animals will suffer a horrific death in the end. Watch 'Earthlings.' Learn the truth."

Dairy Farm: "You're attacking a farm that takes great care of its animals and makes their time on earth the best they can. So please think of the animals before you attack a caring local business."

Like I said this is a real exchange. So how do you think this went? The activist came out swinging, attacked the farm as having no empathy or compassion, and stating that they enjoyed inflicting suffering. If you were a supporter of the farm and this was your first interaction with a vegan, what would your response be? Would it be, "Hey this vegan is right, the farm is a bunch of cruel jerks," or would you feel sorry for the farm? This was not the only response; many others came to post in defense of the farm, responding negatively toward the activist.

At the end of the day, the farm supporters further solidified their views that vegans were "Just a bunch of a-holes" (edited quote), and the farm page filled with new customers eager to support them. The farm then proceeded to delete the majority of negative comments on their page. This is called *failed activism*. What's worse is it had the opposite effect, bolstering support for the farm instead of persuading people not to buy their products. The message is quite clear that if you want to convince someone of your views, criticism will only invoke a negative response and a shutdown of communication. So what do you do? Well, in the same thread, filled with hundreds of negative exchanges between activists and farm supporters, I wrote this review:

"A vegan and former Canadian I wanted to leave a positive review because few farms show as much compassion for their animals as your farm. Factory farming is truly awful, and I'm grateful that small farms such as this one take on the extra burden of allowing their animals the freedom to graze. What a beautiful area as well! While I think that meat and dairy is an unnecessary part of the human diet, I appreciate your hard work to go above and beyond just a basic level of care."

You can see there is no criticism present in the statement of the farm, no condemnation whatsoever. What is present is an appreciation of the good things the farm does do. Now, I know what you might be thinking: *how could you say this farm is compassionate of the animals when they are murdering them in cold blood after a lifetime of abuse!* Yes, there is no doubt that these animals are not living the lives they should be allowed to, and inside I am just as frustrated as you that this farm exploits animals. However, the reality is, as we have seen, just going

18

online and trying to force submission is a poor tactic. So what was the result of my comment? The farm was almost taken aback and responded almost immediately with praise. They thanked me for my support and understanding, which opened the door for me to ask other questions about the future of dairy.

During the exchange, I was able to plant the seed about how expensive it must be to operate as a grass-fed farm, especially with declining milk prices. I also shared with them the story of Elmhurst, a farm that used to be one of the largest dairy companies in New York City, NY, who couldn't make ends meet. If you are not familiar with them, look in the plant-milk section of your favorite grocery store and you'll see their new line of dairy-free milks. Faced with declining profits, they made the jump from failing farm to booming profits by changing their business model. I shared that if they ever wanted to make their exit from the dairy industry, there could be more profitable alternatives. With that, I wished them my best.

I know it seems small, and you might think that they deserve the harsh criticism, but you should remember they are just people trying to make a living. Criticizing their business does nothing but upset them, and as mentioned, got them more customers than they had before! Instead, you want to win your way into the conversation, not simply looking to score points by getting them mad. If you want to have a conversation, it is essential to keep the person or group you are trying to influence from putting up a defensive front. My entire exchange with the farm focused on opening the door and allowing them to hear my comments. If I had said, "Your farm is awful and you need to produce plant-based milks instead," you can guarantee they would have come right back to defend their current practice and strengthen their resolve to continue doing what they are doing. Instead, they are hopefully still wondering if this dairy industry is the best option and looking to Elm-hurst as a prosperous business model.

DON'T CRITICIZE OTHERS

DON'T LET IT TURN INTO AN ARGUMENT

Have you ever won an argument? You may have felt like you did but no one really does. Instead, both people usually leave the exchange angry and even more hardened in their views. As soon as you tell a person "You are wrong," you have already lost the argument because they will do everything they can to keep from being perceived as wrong. The key to staying out of an argument is to realize you are getting into one, and the key phrases that signal you are about to make that mistake are: "That's not right," or "No, you're wrong." Regardless if you are right, moving out of the realm of conversation and into a battle of wits is a sure fire way to accomplish nothing, and it can happen quicker than you think. Here's a perfect example:

Sally: "I don't know why anyone would stop eating meat? Protein is an essential part of the human diet; you have to eat meat."

How would you respond to this? Would you say: "Sally you're an idiot, don't you know that all plants have protein?" I bet you that most vegans would be quick to come back with such a response and show just how much more they know about food and protein than Sally. I admit I used to do this too. How exciting it is to show Sally up and let her know just how wrong she is, right? The result, of course, is that Sally becomes defensive and instead of considering that she might be wrong, she focuses her attention solely on defending herself from your attack.

By telling the other person that they are wrong, you trigger in them the need to protect themselves; you are activating their fight or flight response. Once the person you are talking to is in the fight or flight mode, you can guarantee you have already lost the chance to make an impact; you are in an argument. No matter if you have the best facts, the most compelling story, or fantastic talking points, all of it will be unheard or dismissed as the other person attempts to defend their pride. No one wants to be wrong and will do whatever is necessary to save face, and that's why your approach should never involve trying to best the other person.

So what do you say to Sally? Instead of jumping to prove Sally is wrong, try to find something positive to anchor the discussion on, or at least a middle ground.

You: "Sally, you are totally right about protein; it's essential for humans but where do you think those animals get their protein from?"

Can you see the difference, and how this type of response opens up the discussion rather than invoking a defensive posture? Now you have a variety of places to go to further the discussion. You can talk about how large herbivores get all their protein from plants. You can share how plant protein is a better source since it is free from cholesterol, hormones, and antibiotics. You can continue the discussion any way you like, as long as you keep it from becoming an argument.

Another technique is to say, "I heard otherwise, but maybe I'm wrong. Maybe we can look it up." By saying this, you defuse a potential argument, allow the other person to re-evaluate their stance, and show the other person that you're open-minded. You can also ask some questions about their stance. Many people have strong opinions on topics they know little about; Genetically Modified Organisms, or GMOs, for instance, generate some strong opinions. If someone says that GMOs are bad, you can say, "Well, tell me what you know about GMOs?" By asking some questions about the topic, the other person may realize that they are trying to argue about something they don't really know much about, and that can cause them to reevaluate their stance as well. This opens the door again to say, "Let's look it up together," rather than try to counter their argument.

Now, what if during the conversation you realize that you were wrong about something? Maybe you looked GMOs up and they were terrible, you misquoted an article, or you read something online that turned out to be false. If you find out that you were wrong about something, make sure you admit it quickly and honestly. The last thing you want is to lose credibility, and a sure way to do that is by trying to cover up a misstatement or embellishing the truth. More so, you may open up the conversation by showing that you can admit when you are wrong as it encourages the other person to do so as well.

NEVER SAY "YOU ARE WRONG"

SPEAKING ABOUT FACTS

As a science-loving nerd, I can tell you from my heart there is nothing I love more than a list of awesome research-based facts. In Appendix A, you can find one hundred fast facts to help during your discussions. You might say, "Perfect! I'm going to use these facts right now to convince all my friends and family to go vegan!" That's exactly what I did. The first time I read the World Health Organization report that classified red meat as a Class 2 carcinogen, meaning it probably causes cancer, I thought, *How could anyone continue to eat red meat after learning about this?*[1] Armed with this knowledge, I confronted two of my family members, sure that they would finally realize how horrible eating meat was for their health. Excited, I showed them the study and said, "Look, here is actual proof that red meat causes cancer, just like I said. You both need to quit eating meat; it's making you sick."

So what do you think the response was? Do you think my family members looked at the study and said, "Yes, you're right, we need to make a change"? You probably already know they didn't do that at all. Instead, they both were incredibly fast to say, "It says *probably* causes cancer! Some study this is. *Probably* doesn't mean anything; what a joke." My face could not have looked any more shocked. Here I stood with stone cold proof that red meat causes cancer and they were in complete denial. I further pressed that it was from the International Agency for Research on Cancer (IARC), one of the most prestigious organizations in the world.[1] "Nonsense," they replied. "They don't have a clue; your great-aunt ate meat and she lived well into her nineties." I didn't even know how to reply.

This wasn't the first time I had gotten some pushback from using facts, but it will always be the most memorable. If you read the report from the WHO, there is no doubt that it is accurate and the evidence is compelling; so why the resistance? It's a more in-depth topic than you think and even has a name: the backfire effect. The fact is, facts rarely convince anyone. Instead, they reaffirm existing beliefs or are dismissed as false. In a study by Dartmouth, they found that when confronted with unwelcome facts, people don't just resist new information but "[…] direct factual contradictions can actually strengthen ideologically grounded factual beliefs."[2] What happens is that when you confront someone with new information, in an attempt to defend their preexisting beliefs they will seek out just about any argument to support their stance. That same thing happened when I confronted my family members with the new information about red meat; they immediately started to seek out additional arguments to shore up their position, namely the case of my great-aunt living so long.

That certainly doesn't mean that facts are useless, and I'm just as relieved as you are. So what can you do? Well, you have to get the other person's buy-in *before* you start throwing out facts, or you can bet the other person will be resistant to hearing that new information. Find that common ground and get them agreeing on topics we can all agree on. In the instance of the WHO report, you want them to mentally be ready to accept the fact that red meat is probably a bad thing. The only way that is going to happen is if they already think that red meat is a potentially bad thing. So instead of throwing that fact right out there, you want to get some buy-in by asking the person what they think about it first. For example:

You: "Did you see that new commercial for a one pound hamburger? How does that not make someone sick trying to eat that? I may not eat meat, but that seems excessive, don't you think?"

Them: "Yeah I saw that too. You're right, I'm sure a pound of hamburger isn't good for anyone."

You: "How much do you think is too much?"

Them: "I don't know, probably not that much."

You: "I think you're right! I just read a report from the WHO that encourages people to eat less red meat. I'll send it to you; I'd like to know your thoughts about it."

Them: "Okay, yeah that would be interesting to read."

Now, this is just an example, but it was to make the point that once you get someone headed in a certain direction, they want to continue. The other person is now receptive to new information because it supports their viewpoint. One more example. If you have someone that loves hotdogs and you say to them, "You shouldn't eat hotdogs because they cause cancer," what do you think they are going to say back? They will probably dismiss your claim or ignore it because you are directly attacking their love of hotdogs. However, if you say to them instead, "How healthy do you think hot dogs are?" How do you think they would respond? I'm guessing they will be at least be semi-honest and admit that they are not the healthiest thing in the world. Using that opportunity, you can then add in, "Yeah I agree with you! I read that they might even cause cancer." Who doesn't like to be right? Not only have you made them feel good about their current knowledge, but you've also got that new information in the door without any resistance.

If you want to use facts you have to make sure that they support a viewpoint the other person already holds, or they will work to defend their current beliefs at all costs. No one wants to think their actions or thoughts are wrong, so find some common ground to build a new way of thinking rather than trying to destroy an existing thought structure. By using this technique, you allow the person to see the facts for what they are and bypass their natural resistance to new information.

FACTS ONLY CONVINCE PEOPLE WHO ARE WILLING TO HEAR THEM

SHOW APPRECIATION

Biologically, humans are physiologically designed to pursue activities that reward them, usually in the form of the release of the chemical dopamine. Dopamine causes a feel-good sensation, stimulates the brain's reward system, and typically encourages a person to perform the activity or action again. The release of this chemical can come from a variety of external stimuli, but the outcome is the same: they want to experience more good feelings. So use it to your advantage! Get the other person feeling good about themselves. The more positive feedback you give, the more the other person will want to continue receiving it. We just saw how damaging criticism was, so what should you do instead? If you want to get someone's attention, try complimenting them.

It's essential for the compliment to be thoughtful, honest, and sincere. Have you ever been in a mall or walking down a street corner and someone at a sales booth tries to grab your attention? Most of us have experienced this type of direct sales, and from it, you should have a pretty good idea of what not to do to get someone's attention. Let's look at two scenarios where a vendor is attempting to get you to try and eventually buy a backscratcher.

Scenario One

Imagine, if you will, walking down a sidewalk full of shops and Sally, a well-dressed young person, is standing in front of the shop ahead of you with a backscratcher in hand. As you walk by, the person looks at you and says:

"Hey, would you like to try a backscratcher?"

You're probably already shaking your head no, and that is incredibly common. This is the typical sales pitch, right? It's very impersonal, verbally intrusive, and almost certain to fail the majority of the time. It almost has a similar ring if you were to shout "Go vegan" at someone, right? You can tell right away the vendor could care less about you, and they are only concerned with the sale of the product. As soon as you see the person selling the item, if you're like me, you're probably thinking about crossing the street to avoid the conversation altogether.

So what does this have to do with convincing others to go vegan? You may not be on the street selling a product, but the scenario is more similar than you might think. You might think people will want to hear your fantastic message of veganism, love for animals, and health benefits, but the reality is the other person is probably wanting to run to the other side of the street. You might have all the facts, a great personal story, or phenomenal recipes to share, but at the end of the day, others see you as just another person trying to sell them something, even though there's no money changing hands. What makes them so similar is that there is no personal connection and no attempt to say you are important to me as a person, not just as a potential sale. So what can you do to not come off as just trying to sell something? Let's let Sally try again.

"Excuse me, Hi! I'm Sally, and I'm giving out free back scratches if you have thirty seconds; it's a wonderful experience!

How do you feel now? Do you have thirty seconds to spare? I'm willing to bet at least some people would say yes. What changed, though? Sally is still offering a free back scratch. I'm sure you've caught on that what changed was that she is no longer offering a product but an experience. She shifted her pitch from focusing on the product to concentrating on how she could make a personal connection by sharing an experience and making the other person feel valued and important.

John Dewey was an American philosopher and psychologist and was one of most profound intellectuals of his day. One of his most profound revelations was that the deepest urge in human nature is "The desire to be important."[3] The desire to be great is almost as important as basic human needs such as health, food, sleep, sex, and security. In short, it is a powerful tool that you can use to de-arm the defense mechanism that you will encounter as you attempt to bring up the topic of a vegan lifestyle. For example, you have a friend who is considering buying a down pillow.

Scenario Two

As a vegan, you know that the animals down manufacturers exploit are subject to excruciating pain, and often death, from the removal of their feathers. You, knowing how terrible this industry is, want your friend to realize what they are contributing to by buying this pillow, so you say:

"Rob, don't you know that this pillow is the result of birds having their feathers ripped out? If you buy that, you are a horrible person that supports animal abuse!"

Okay, maybe that's a bit overdramatic, but it gets the point across. Immediately Rob is going to put his guard up and attempt to defend his choice to get the pillow. He might respond that he has always used down pillows, or that they are the only kind he can sleep on due to a bad neck. Whatever the response, you can almost be sure that it will be one that downplays the animal violence and supports his choice to purchase the pillow. What other option does he have after being called an animal abuser? Rob feels the need to defend himself and his reputation, and will mentally move to a position that people who buy down pillows are not horrible but good people because he considers himself to be a good person; who wouldn't? Thus, by trying to shame someone into making an ethical choice, the opposite has happened, and they have become hardened in their decision; this is a psychological concept called Reactance.

Reactance occurs when a person adopts or strengthens a view or attitude that is contrary to what was intended usually due to someone taking away their choices. Also, by demonizing something or an activity, it can often take on a forbidden-fruit type appearance that makes it seem more appealing. Bottom line, it further shows that techniques like criticism and shaming a choice don't have a high success rate. What can you do? Show appreciation for their decisions and lead them to a better choice.

"Rob, I didn't know you were such a pillow connoisseur. I read a lot of people that use down pillows are switching to bamboo because the feel is similar and it's a more sustainable source of material. Have you ever tried one?"

Wow, right? Do you think Rob will make the switch to bamboo? I'm guessing it's very likely for two reasons: his guard is down after complimenting his desire to use quality pillows, and he has an alternative that a lot of people are switching to. Rob is open to the change because it seems appealing, and if you were to mention some of the abuses in the down industry, it might have a real impact because the discussion is no longer "You shouldn't" but "You love great pillows, and this one is even better."

The main takeaway is that everyone appreciates a sincere compliment and feeling valued. By saying something nice or going out of your way to do nice things, you put the other person in a positive and receptive state of mind.

MAKE THEM FEEL VALUED TO LOWER THEIR DEFENSES

USE HUMOR

Remember when you were young and your parents would come up to you and say, "We need to talk." Do you recall that stomach-sinking feeling that you did something wrong? No one likes this type of confrontational approach, yet so many people approach others this way. Instead of making the conversation inviting or appealing, they immediately pounce at the first opportunity to bring up the topic of veganism, without any regard for the other person. If you do this, you can guarantee the person you're trying to talk to will be looking for the nearest exit to get out of an uncomfortable situation. So how do you make the situation less intrusive? Instead, relax, don't push the issue, and use some humor.

On social media you will often find memes or other jests saying something to the tune of, "This is why I'm not vegan," and underneath will be a variety of meat pictures. I had a good friend of mine post something similar, but instead of a meme he had a picture of his dinner, a steak with a baked potato covered with cheese, and above it, "This is Why I'm Not Vegan!" In the comments section, his friends posted a variety of comments, most showing support for the comment with responses like, "Yummm, that looks good." So what would you do in this instance? I can tell you what my first thought was. I wanted to jump right on that thread and unleash a slew of vegan memes of my own and fill it with articles showing how unhealthy that steak was. I wanted him to see that he was contributing to his risk of heart disease and cancer for something as fleeting as taste. I wanted to do all of this, but I didn't. I knew that if I came out swinging, all of the others on the thread would likely do the same, posting picture after picture of various animal products and abuse in response. I'm sure you have seen this play out many times if you are active on social media.

A great way to make an impact in a hostile environment is to use a bit of humor to open the discussion, so you don't appear to be a threat to the established group dynamic. That's precisely what I did in the case of my friend. On the same thread, I posted the comment, "Vegans don't know what they're missing out on," and put a picture of the new Beyond

Meat sausages, cooked without the packaging. The others in the group were accepting of the comment because they had no idea that I was vegan. When my friend saw the comment he immediately put a comment asking why I was posting meat pictures: "Dude, did you give up being vegan?" When I let on that the sausages were vegan, my friend and the fellow commenters realized that they had been had. They continued to make a couple of comments about how they probably don't taste as good, but the gig was already up. They had to sit back and laugh a bit because the picture fooled them. More importantly, it allowed them to make the connection that vegan food isn't some weird tofu thing, but something that looks every bit as good as the steak my friend posted. On top of that, I got one comment that was exactly what I was hoping for: "Hey, that does look pretty good."

The point to this story is that you can use humor to disarm a hostile crowd or an individual, on social media or in person. Is someone's steak dinner a joke? Of course not, it's horrible, and the suffering behind it is real, but you have to look at the long game. The goal is to use humor to open up the discussion, so you have the opportunity to make an impact rather than get immediately shut out.

If you are naturally funny or quick on your feet, this could come easily to you; however, if you are like me, I like to have some go-to laughs already in my bag so I'm not trying to come up with something on the spot. For instance, when someone tries to make a case that I am going to get seriously ill from a lack of protein, I quickly flip that around and say, "It's too late, I already died months ago and have been living as a zombie ever since." This would be a great time to throw in a great zombie impersonation and say, "I need grains." Okay, that's pretty corny, but just like that, you have disarmed that negative comment and opened up space to have a real conversation about a plant-based diet.

USE HUMOR TO OPEN THE DISCUSSION

PRAISE AND BE COMPASSIONATE

While it's natural to want the other person to go vegan right away, it's just as important to remember that most do so over time. A whopping 68 percent of people that become vegan either went vegetarian first or did so incrementally (Chart 2.1).[4] The amount of time it takes could be a month, a year, or longer, and that should be understandable since the vast majority of us have been meat-eaters all our lives. Like any change in life, it's going to take some getting used to, and they are probably going to have some setbacks as well. Knowing this, you not only need to cheer for their successes, but also be compassionate about their failures along the way. How you react could be the difference between someone becoming the next animal advocate or someone that says, "Yeah, I tried that vegan thing and it's overrated."

Chart 2.1: Transitioning to Vegan[4]

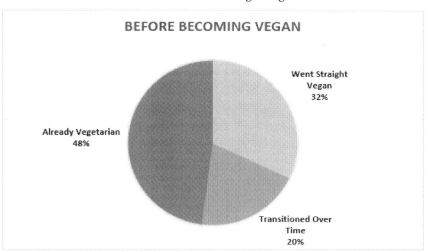

If the other person messes up or, as it's often called, "falls off the wagon," keep your cool and let it go. For most of us, eating meat has been a lifetime of conditioning, and it takes a while to get those reward pathways rerouted from cheese and burgers to firing for crispy tofu and BBQ jackfruit. If your friend gives in and has some cheese, don't shame them morally; instead, help them find a plant-based alternative that they can go to next time. I don't how many times I've seen someone say, "I messed up and had some cheese," only to have tons of vegans jump on them saying, "You need to watch some dairy videos," or "This is a vegan group, eating cheese isn't vegan!" Those kinds of comments only make the other person intimidated and not want to be vegan. After all, who wants to be part of a group that attacks their own? A better comment to make is, "It's okay, we all mess up and it takes some time. Have you tried Violife cheese? Get some of that and keep it in the fridge for when you really want something cheesy."

For the successes, never miss an opportunity to share some praise. If your friend says, "After our talks, you've convinced me… I'm giving up beef!" you might want to say, "The other animals suffer just as much, why don't you give up everything!" I was the same way. I wanted everyone to go vegan today, but the reality is if you push their timeline, you're likely to endanger any progress they may have made so far. So no matter how small the change (giving up hot dogs, switching to plant-milks, etc.) make sure you show your excitement, your joy, and your gratitude. Make it a big deal; make it something your friend or family member will want to continue doing!

A way to have an even more significant impact is to use their name as well. One of the most wonderful things people love to hear is their name. When you praise someone, you have much more impact when you also put their name in the comment. For example, "Jake, I'm proud you gave up beef." Using their name not only gets their attention better but has a more personal impact than just a casual comment.

PRAISE EVERY CHANGE

NON-VERBAL COMMUNICATION

It's well known that your body language often conveys more information than the words you speak. While your body language expresses visible signs of emotion, it can also communicate subtle messages as well that are unconsciously picked up by the other person. That's why it's important to use the right body language to give the other person a positive vibe during any kind of interaction.

Before we get into how to adjust your body language, I want to give you an idea of what kind of impact negative body language can have, and I can't think of a better example than a stereotypical vegan. Do you remember before you went vegan what your perception of vegans, or even vegetarians, was? I know there will be some exceptions, but for the majority of us we probably envisioned what the media has portrayed: angry, in your face, shouting, judgmental, preachy, etc. You may even know other vegans that fit this stereotype. Now imagine yourself a non-vegan, and a person comes up to you in an angry manner, wearing a "meat is murder" shirt and holding a tablet with a slaughter video playing, and they are about to speak to you for the first time about being vegan. Before they even say a word, what do you think? Is this a person you want to talk to, or do you want to run at full speed for the exit? I know that I would be the first one out the door, yet this happens all the time.

You might be thinking, "Well, that's not me; I don't participate in militant demonstrations like that." I would ask you to take a quick look at your social media. Is your Facebook page covered in vegan posts? Do you have slaughter videos and pictures littering your timeline? Do all of your selfies say "Go Vegan" on them? Are you continually re-tweeting vegan tweets? As a vegan, I would probably love your social media accounts, but just like the scenario above, your non-verbal expressions are likely to put you at a disadvantage when it comes to spreading your message. It's a tough pill to swallow, or at least it was for me. Your family, your friends, and your acquaintances may not even give you the chance to make a case, tuning out before you even say a word. So what can you do instead?

One important thing you can do when you are thinking of engaging someone is reduce anything that might be highly polarizing. This could be anything from mellowing out your social media account to being a bit more friendly to everyone, or opting for that plain tee-shirt vs. the "Not your Mom, not your milk" shirt. In essence, you don't want to shut down the conversation before it even gets started. Even better, if you can match culture or vibe your target audience, your thoughts and opinions are much more likely to be well received.

People like others that express positive attributes and who share similarities to themselves. We trust and want to engage with others that look like us, act like us, and share our interests. There's probably no better example of this in action than during a Presidential election in the United States. Commonly referred to as code-switching, if you watch any Presidential campaign move throughout the many states, you may notice that the candidate's speech and mannerisms often change to match the culture of the audience. In 2008, former secretary of state Hillary Clinton and former Senator John Edwards were both cast into the spotlight for suddenly acquiring a southern accent while giving speeches during their campaigns. Former President Lyndon Johnson would bring out a "full drawl" when he campaigned as a Senator in his home state of Texas. In contrast, former senator Mitt Romney was criticized for not code-switching by John McWhorter, a linguist at the Manhattan Institute, saying "[He] will not go anywhere because he cannot be verbally warm."[5]

You may not be running for office, but the way you speak, your mannerisms, your public image, and your posture have a big impact on your ability to convince others. Presidential candidates know this. What they are doing is synchronizing their body language to match the person or people they are talking too. It may sound silly, but it is one of the fastest ways to build trust and open communication with other people. Look at how the other person is standing. Do they have their arms folded? Are they sitting in a chair? Try doing the same. Don't make a blatant thing out of it, like changing your body position exactly when they do, but ever so gently aim to make your body language match that of your audience. What you are saying non-verbally is that "I am with you, I am like you."

In the same way, your speech and tone should match that of the person. Do they talk slowly or is their speech at a faster pace? Do they speak loudly with energy, or do they talk softly and carefully? As best you can, and without trying to fake it, try to match their mood, the pace of their speech, and the energy of the conversation. Not only does this work in person, but it also works on the phone and even online. When you type responses to others, try to use the same type of verbiage and a similar length of comments. If they use a lot of emojis, throw some in there as well. If they use ALL CAPS... maybe consider not doing that, but do your best. One last note: other things like swearing, derogatory comments, or offensive slang are undoubtedly things you would not want to match in any discussion.

Here are some more things you can do to help non-verbally improve your ability to communicate:

SMILE! I'm sure you can guess that smiling is one of the best and easiest non-verbal cues you can use to put someone at ease. Not only does smiling add warmth and an aura of confidence, but it also makes people trust what you are saying, and the more genuine the smile, the more others believe you.[6] So when you're talking to others, and the situation allows it, make sure to smile and use it as a means to shift your whole body into a reflection of positivity.

Open your hands. The next time you see a political debate, take a look at their hands. More times than not, you will see political candidates have their hands open, even in instances where they are just standing around on stage. If you've ever noticed it, you might have thought that it's kind of a weird thing to be standing around like that. It's a very deliberate tactic to show they have "nothing to hide." Now I'm sure most have a lot to hide; after all, they are politicians! But the concept works, and they employ it for just that reason, as should you. You don't have to be awkward about it but if you can remember while in any kind of discussion, take a second to look down at your hands. Are they open and welcoming? Or are they balled up in a fist from a confrontational discussion? Keep them loose and relaxed.

Lastly, make eye contact. Eye contact lets the other person know you are engaged in the discussion, and more importantly it helps to convey the emotion behind what you are saying. It helps to build trust and is a simple and easy way to connect with another person if you do it right. What do I mean by *do it right*? Don't make it awkward; that is to say, don't stare someone down; no one wants to be just stared at. I guarantee if you just eyeball someone for a couple of minutes, going vegan will be the furthest thing from their mind as they are wondering what the heck is wrong with you. An easy way to keep from being awkward is to maintain eye contact for around five seconds at a time and about 50 percent of the time. Doing this will ensure you are staying engaged and connected without being overwhelming.

DON'T FORGET ABOUT BODY LANGUAGE

BE A GREAT LISTENER

Have you ever had a conversation with someone and they continually cut you off or began talking over you? How did it make you feel? I start to lose interest very quickly, and instead, I focus more on trying to get a word in than on the topic of discussion. The more knowledge you acquire about vegan issues, the more you are going to want to share every bit of that knowledge with the other person in a long, rambling lecture. You want to make sure that doesn't happen, and an easy way to prevent that is to let the other person do more of the talking.

Letting the other person talk shows it's not a one-sided conversation and that you care about their opinion. While they are talking, be an active listener; nod your head or verbally acknowledge if you think they are right about something or make a good point, even if you don't agree with it. This not only helps to form a relationship of mutual respect but creates a higher likelihood that when you talk and share your thoughts, they too will listen and agree with your points as well. A great way to let them do most of the talking is to ask questions, and we will talk about that next.

One last thing: don't interrupt the person you are speaking to, even if you disagree with what they are saying. Just like you don't want to be cut off, allow them the chance to talk. Interrupting them can be seen as an attack or make the other person feel like that's a topic they need to defend. Instead, listen patiently and when it's your turn to talk you are more likely to be afforded the same courtesy.

LET THEM DO MOST OF THE TALKING AND DON'T INTERRUPT

THE SOCRATIC METHOD

If you take anything away from this book, it should be that while you can influence those around you, the choice to go vegan will ultimately be theirs. You will not be able to shame someone into going vegan, and aggressive methods may have a short-term effect, but it's unlikely to have any lasting change. They have to make the connection on their own, and the process may take days, months, or years. So how do you allow for self-change versus trying to push the issue? The basic answer is to lead the conversation where you want them to go, and a great way to do that is by asking questions.

One favorite method for using questions to break down beliefs is called the Elenchus, or the Socratic Method. This method is named after the great Socrates who lived in the 5th century B.C. The process itself consists of primarily using questions to get the other person to think critically about the reason they hold certain beliefs, rather than trying for force feed them answers. If you have ever seen videos of James Aspey, Earthling Ed, or others engaged in activism, you'll see they often use this method as a way to get a conversation started and force the other person to question why it is they eat and use animal products. I often use it as well, especially while doing public activism, as it helps to guide the discussion and elicit familiar responses. Why it works is that it makes the discussion about the other person, rather than a one-sided lecture, gets them to participate in the reasoning process, and helps them to draw their own conclusions.

While this method is gaining traction among vegan activists, it's used by literally thousands of others for the same purpose. An important note is that the Socratic Method is *not* just asking random questions, or loaded questions for that matter. Instead, just as we talked about before with using facts, you want to use the questions to build a new way of thinking.

The basic premises is to build upon the other person's moral framework by asking questions that get a *yes* answer; this is sometimes also called the yes ladder. You want to get them saying yes, because once you do, people tend to want to keep saying yes! For instance: "Do you think that animal cruelty is wrong?" Just about anyone you talk to is going to say, "Yes." That response allows you to lead the discussion to the conclusion that killing animals for food is also animal cruelty. Here's a basic example of how this would work:

You: "Do you think that animal cruelty is wrong?"

Them: "Um, yes, of course."

You: "Okay, great, I agree as well; it's awful. Do you eat animals?"

Them: "Yes, I do."

You: "Do you think killing an animal is cruel?"

Them: "Um, I suppose there would be some cruelty to it; you are killing them."

You: "It seems like a cruel thing to do to me as well. Do you think that killing animals for food then is animal cruelty?"

Them: "I guess so, but we have to kill them, so we have something to eat."

You: "Are there other things we could maybe eat instead?"

Them: "Yes, I guess we could."

I think you get the gist. The main focus is that you want to keep the other person saying yes and coming to logical conclusions on their own that lead from their moral foundation to the conclusion you are trying to reach. In doing this you are no longer going directly head-on with their established beliefs, but circumventing them entirely by creating new ones built from their morals. By being included in the thought process, they can question their own actions without feeling it necessary to defend themselves. Oh, and if they do say "yes," to some serious questions, that would be the time to throw out facts to support their new found realization.

For many more examples of how to use the Socratic Method, you can check out some activist videos, look up the method on YouTube or Google, or head to the library; it's only been around for 2500 years.

ASK QUESTIONS TO LEAD THE DISCUSSION AND KEEP THEM SAYING "YES"

CHAPTER 3
FAMILY, FRIENDS, AND EVERYONE

OKAY, YOU NOW have the foundation, so how do we inspire change?

First, I hate to break this to you, but your friends and especially your family will be the hardest people to convince—much more so than just someone off the street. Even the great Gary Yourofsky, one of the most well-known animal activists, said, "I've had virtually no success with friends and family members [...], they're like the toughest people in the world," in an interview with Bite Size Vegan.[1] It's odd and unfair, but there is a natural disposition for those who know you best to believe others outside of your circle and to be hesitant to trust what you are saying to be true. For your friends, it might be their resistance to your personal change if you weren't vegan before they met you. For your family, it could be a mixture of judgment about how they raised you or never forgetting all the times you were wrong or made a mistake. There are a lot of reasons, but the main point is that your relationships with others also tend to make change harder.

The good news is that it can be overcome, but you will also have to be a bit more strategic with those that know you best to drop their pre-established defenses. If you demand your friends and family go vegan, they are sure to resist it. However, if you say, "I want to help you…" lose weight or reverse your heart disease, you will be surprised to get a much more positive response.

Second, before we get into a bit of the *how-to* for helping people to go vegan, I'd like to introduce you to an acronym I use to prepare myself for discussions called DEAL. DEAL stands for:

D - Describe why it is important to *them*. You probably have a lot of reasons you want the other person to go vegan, but you will need to provide them a reason as to why they should consider making a change beyond "I want you to." Remember, you have to make *them* want to make the change. A good word to use is *because*. For instance: "Hey, you like soup, right? I thought you might be interested in this recipe *because* you love soup." Using because can help you figure out why it's important to them.

E - Expect there will be resistance and a feeling of judgment. You're asking them to make a significant change in their life, so expect that most people will be resistant to the request and be understanding that this reaction is normal.

A - Answer objections. Remember all the questions you had when you first went vegan? The other person is going to have just as many or more. You don't need to be the expert on every topic, but you should at least be ready to answer questions or direct them to an appropriate resource.

L - Leave on a positive note. The most important part of the DEAL is to end every discussion positively. Don't be the person that gets mad or storms off in frustration. Do your best to make your case for going vegan, but remember the other person is not your enemy. Even if they reject your answers or your reasoning, thank them for at least being willing to listen, and make sure they feel their contributions to the discussion are valued, not just rejected.

I'm not the biggest fan of acronyms, but they do help, especially when you get asked the same question over and over: "Why should I?" It gives you some framework to know what's coming your way and some time to prepare yourself. This way you will be able to provide some solid answers that will leave a lasting impression rather than a quick response that leaves the other person thinking you don't know what you are talking about.

YOUR PARTNER/SPOUSE

When you commit to go vegan, the person that will surely be the most affected will be your spouse, partner, or significant other. If you were already together, you were probably used to doing everything together, such as going to movies, walking in the park, and of course, eating out or at home. Now that you have made the switch, your partner is indeed left wondering what that means for them. Will they ever get to eat at a restaurant with you again? Will you starve to death from a lack of protein while they look on in horror? Will you become a roaming hippie, forgoing showers and protesting on the side of the road? Even if you were vegan before meeting your partner, the questions will be much of the same, as well as their adjustment to your lifestyle.

However, now that your partner has finally come to terms that you are vegan, no doubt you're ready to break the most obvious news, which is that you want them to go vegan too. The range of reactions is broad and can be as exciting as, "Hey, you know, I was interested in eating less meat too," to "If you're going to be a preachy vegan then I want to end the relationship." Regardless of the response, there are a lot of things you can do to encourage the transition, and likely even help them to go vegan as well. What should you do? Well, let's take a walk through the DEAL method.

Describe why it's important to them
Partner: "Hey, I'm looking in the fridge, and there's nothing but vegetables in here. I told you that I'm not doing that vegan thing, so what am I supposed to eat?"

You: "There is a lot more than vegetables in there, but because you said the other day that you wanted to get back in shape, I got you the best foods to help you do that."

Expect there will be resistance and a feeling of judgment
Partner: "I wanted to lose a couple of pounds, not starve to death!"

You: "You won't starve to death; what's your concern?"

Answer objections

Partner: "Well, I need lean protein, like chicken and fish, to get in shape; everyone knows all the best athletes eat lots of protein."

You: "Well, what I got you was 'lean protein.' I got lots of beans and nuts that are not only high in protein but in nutrition too. Chicken and fish are loaded with saturated fat and cholesterol, how is that part of an athletic diet?"

Leave on a positive note

Partner: "Hmm, I didn't think about the saturated fat. I don't know, though; I feel like I'm not going to get enough protein from eating salads."

You: "You will get tons of protein, and I have an app on my phone we can use to track it so you can see exactly what your protein intake is. I would be so excited if you just give it a try; you could really like it!"

That is the basis of the DEAL method, to provide a general idea of conversation progression and to allow you to think ahead a bit on what topics might come up and how to lead the discussion to a positive end rather than let it turn into an argument. That said, this scenario is just a small bit of what the conversation could dive into, and we will get into responses to objections later on, as well as a whole list of reasons you can give to go vegan.

Here are some additional ideas to help your partner transition:

Be the chef

Now for some good news. As their partner, you have a pretty significant impact when it comes to changing their mind and habits. Since your likely around each other every day, your ability to continually drive the issue is second to none, as long as you don't let it take the form of nagging or criticism. For instance, if you are the chef of your home, you can easily make a case for going vegan almost without saying a word. Many partners will start by making vegan meals, and that in itself is enough to get the other person interested in plant-based food, at least at home, just based on them not wanting to go through the hassle of cooking another meal. I say this from experience because, as mentioned before, when I was the chef of my home, no way did I want to prepare two separate meals. So when my spouse decided to make the change to a plant-based diet, I did what made sense to me and cooked a single meal, and I just added extra stuff—which didn't last long as I found how good recipes could be without animal products.

You may be tempted to say, "No animal products in the house, period!" and while other hardcore vegans will applaud you, it will likely cause the opposite reaction in your partner, who will feel forced into the decision. Remember what I said in the beginning about how they have to want to make the change, and they need some time to do that. I get it, and I 100 percent realize the reaction of many would be, "How can you actually suggest this?" My response is to look at the long game. I would never suggest you ditch your morals, but if the tradeoff was losing a partner, and potentially the chance to help them go vegan, over not being semi-flexible to allow them to slowly transition, it seems reasonable to be accommodating. Just as you chose to go vegan on your terms, they will have to make a choice on theirs, meaning, trying to strong-arm the decision will likely cause increased opposition, which is precisely what you don't want.

However, just because you allow the other person to keep eating animal products doesn't mean you have to promote it. If you are the one still having to cook them for your partner, you can make those products less appealing by serving them plain. Instead of adding all those plant seasonings, cook it with nothing added and leave the all the natural trimmings like veins and fat attached. It might allow the other person to see what it is they are actually eating, and without seasoning, most animal products are pretty disgusting. Meanwhile, cook special things for yourself and make them seem like a forbidden fruit; things like crispy tofu and buffalo tempeh. Saying phrases like, "Oh this, you probably wouldn't like this vegan thing, so I made you that instead," uses reverse psychology to arise a desire not to be left out. Making your partner want to try something is the key to getting them interested.

Make it hip

Let's face it, until recently vegans and vegetarians were excluded from the national discussion. Vegan was a word you never heard of, and vegetarians were weird hippies that ate grass and didn't bathe. I'm sure you can see the point that you will have to make the concept more attractive than long-standing stereotypes have painted it. That said, what's not to be excited about: having better health, being kind and compassionate, and helping to save the Earth! That's the kind of excitement you will have to convey to break down some of those mental barriers your partner likely has.

Celebrities are an excellent way to make a case for veganism as a growing hip movement. There are hundreds of well-known vegans across every genre of music, art, and movies, as well as in sports and popular hobbies. Beatles lovers, for instance, are sure to take note that Paul McCartney is vegan and a very avid supporter of animal rights. Rocker Joan Jett and pop stars Miley Cyrus, Sia, and Ariana Grande are all vegans as well. Peter Dinklage from the highly popular Game of Thrones is also vegan. Everywhere you look, celebrities are making the change to a compassionate lifestyle, and each time a new celebrity joins the list, it makes front page news in magazines and on social media, as was the case when Beyoncé announced that she was moving towards a vegan diet. While these transitions positively energize the vegan movement, don't forget to use the momentum to your advantage by showing your partner the good news too.

Ever been to a VegFest? VegFests are popping up all over the world and are an easy way to get your partner to see how popular being vegan is, as well as to try out some fantastic food. There are usually lots of speakers and events going on that showcase why animal rights are such an important topic. Bottom line, people generally like festivals, and it's a great way to have a good time while exposing your partner to a world with which they might not be familiar.

Finally, the number of vegans across the world is also a strong signal that it's not just a fad, but a global movement. In the U.S. only 0.5 percent of the population was vegan in 2008, from a study by Harris

Interactive. By 2017 the percent of the U.S. vegan population has sky-rocketed to over 6 percent according to GlobalData.[2] The U.S. isn't alone either. In the U.K. the percent of vegans has increased by 350 percent compared to a decade ago, according to the Vegan Society, and is now at a whopping 7 percent of the population. In Australia, the percentage is even higher at a massive 9.3 percent from the latest figures put out by Roy Morgan Research.[2] Veganism is no longer the micro-niche it used to be. It is a global force for good, poised to change societies across the world.

Make it personal

Your partner needs to know that this is not just some fad for you and that it's a permanent change with a lifetime commitment. At some point, you will inevitably be asked if you are really in this vegan thing for the long haul. This is a fantastic opportunity to make it personal, and bring out the heavy weapons of the vegan arsenal if the timing is right. I say if the timing is right because it may not be the right time early on to show very graphic videos of slaughterhouses or the abuse that goes on at fur farms. If you show videos like that very early on, there is a fair chance that they will not have the intended impact. Without some breaking down of the perception that eating animals is normal, your partner may watch a documentary like *Earthlings* and be put off or rationalize that it is a necessary activity. Others may be so shocked and disturbed that they refuse to watch such a documentary. The same is true for documentaries on environmental impacts, like *Cowspiracy*. You have to break down those barriers beforehand, or they will mentally dismiss the information. So how can you make the most significant impact with your partner? After you have given them some time to go through the DEAL process, and after they have had the opportunity to see some of the positives of a vegan lifestyle—for instance, some new foods or interest in better health—you can make it personal.

Everyone has different reasons for going vegan, and it's up to you to make a case for why you did and get them interested in the resources you think will have a significant impact. As alluded to with *Earthlings*, seeing the actual raw footage of a working slaughterhouse or fur farm is earth-shattering for many people, and enough to have a lasting impact. For others, documentaries like *What the Health* can make a difference because the majority of people are shocked to learn how embedded the meat and dairy industry are in their lives through advertising and media. The best resource to use is one that addresses what is important to your partner, and no one should know them better than you. However, if you show them a video or let them hear a speech and they respond negatively, don't get discouraged. Everyone is different, and it may take several tries to find something that has the right impact.

Give space for change

So you've talked to your partner, you've introduced them to some new foods, and you showed them the best documentaries. Now what? It's time to give them some space to think for themselves and make their own decision. As mentioned before, you want your partner to make the change for themselves, so you need to give them room for growth to happen. How do you know when you should provide space? Honestly, it's going to be different for everyone, but generally speaking, it should be after a significant breakthrough. If you can see that you have made a lasting impact and your partner can understand where you are coming from and why it's important to you, then it's time to back off. Seriously, not ten minutes or a couple hours, but give them several days. Another good indicator would be if they happen to ask you questions that are no longer objectionable but instead are information seeking, such as "Where do you buy tempeh?" or "What veggies have the most protein?" Now your job is to be a resource, a guide, and, most importantly, a cheerleader.

YOUR PARENTS (OR GRANDPARENTS)

While you have a fair shot at getting your partner to go vegan, your parents are a much harder audience and may be the toughest, especially if you are young. Unlike your partner (if you have one), with whom you likely had to reconcile a lot of differences to be together, your family holds its own culture to be of supreme value, and you've probably had a part in forming that culture. Every family has cherished things they do for holidays, long-standing traditions that are repeated by each genera- tion, and a family identity that has developed throughout the years. You can guarantee that many of those traditions and celebrations involve food, and, unless you happened to grow up in a vegan household, they likely include a variety of meat products—most of which are the main attraction. The typical stars of holidays are main courses like turkey, ham, chicken wings, tamales, etc., usually paired with favorites like Grandma's famous pie and Dad's special 7-layer dip. These dishes are not just food for the holidays, but they are part of the fabric of many fami- lies, and you can expect that trying to make a radical change will be met with confrontation. Dad will be wondering why all of a sudden you are too good to eat his dip, and the kids may be resentful that you no longer want to make that special Thanksgiving meal. So what can you do?

First, you should probably realize that unless your parents have seri- ous health issues going on, or even maybe if they do, convincing them to change their habits is going to be exceedingly difficult. Of all the people I've talked to and had discussions with, none have been as resistant and opposed to change as my parents. I would easily argue that if you can make your parents go vegan, you can get just about anyone too. So why are they so challenging? Well, because they know best, right? They raised you, and since you were born, they made decisions based on a mixture of how their parents raised them and information available at the time.

That said, the information available at that time is at least decades old, if not several decades, depending on the age of your parents. When they grew up, veganism was likely unheard of, and the food pyramid was probably the go-to source for nutritional information. Everyone knew that you needed animal protein for growing muscles and milk for developing bones. What I'm trying to say is that just as you've had to overcome much of the misinformation out there, it will be all the more challenging for your parents to do the same, because they have habits built over a lifetime. So realize when you say that they need to give up meat and dairy and that it's unhealthy, you are in essence saying, "You did a bad job at raising me (and my siblings, if applicable) and most of your life you have been eating garbage and abusing animals." Wow, right! Is it true? Well, yeah, it is, knowing how bad meat and dairy are for you, but the more significant point is that telling them to go vegan has a much more emotional impact than simply just swapping to almond milk.

When it comes to conditioning, few have as much buy-in as my Mom (sorry, Mom). First, let me say that my Mom is a compassionate and caring person who would do anything for you and has adopted more animals in need than most. Obviously, I love her to death and care a great deal about her, and as such, I wanted desperately to transition her to a whole-foods, plant-based diet. Honestly, when I first set out to do that, I thought it would be an easy task. After all, she loves and even rescues animals, and back when I first started eating organic foods, it was because she was the one that had first suggested it. What I didn't expect was that it would be such a monumental challenge.

Like many other people, my parents separated when I was young, and for much of my young life, I lived with my Mom. Even though we didn't have much money, she always did her best to feed me healthy and nutritious meals. Usually, that consisted of the typical three-way segmented plate of a veggie, a starch, and an animal-based protein. She did everything right, and according to the national health guidelines, she was a rockstar. As far as health was concerned, I never really had many issues, at least no more than the typical kid. By all measures, she succeeded as a parent, and likewise, so did her parents. So now years later when I came to her and said I'm vegan now, and you need to be as well, you can understand there was a great deal of resistance.

When I wasn't living with my Mom, I lived with my Dad. Some of my fondest memories growing up are holiday meals with my Dad. My Dad isn't a professional chef, but of all the meals I've ever had, none are, or will ever be, as good as the dishes my Dad has made over the years. I know I'm not alone, and I'm sure that you have that one family member (or members) that makes the most amazing meals. For me, my Dad's best dishes always came out during the holidays, specifically Thanksgiving and Christmas. Although I, like all vegans, look at food differently now, I still have a strong attachment to those meals he made. I won't get into the details of the meals for the sake of the animals, which isn't necessary anyway, because the longing for those meals has nothing to do with the food itself. Instead, the attachment is deeply rooted in the comfort of something unique and familiar, as well as the tradition that my Dad created by having the same meal each year to celebrate the holidays.

Nothing can describe the disappointment both my Dad and I felt when I told him that I would no longer be eating meat. Maybe you can relate. I had effectively ended the tradition, not only for us but for my daughter as well. It wasn't easy to tell my Dad that. Change is never easy, and it didn't go over well when I suggested we change the tradition to no longer include meat.

My point of sharing both these stories is that, while you have the best of intentions, it's not an easy thing to go up to your parents and tell them you're vegan and they need to be vegan as well. Your parents have a lot of personal objections that are unique from others you will engage with, and it's important to consider these objections before trying to convince them to start making changes in their life. One last consideration is that often the challenge isn't just to convince one parent, but two at the same time. If your parents are married, either to each other or remarried, you will likely be trying to win over two parents at the same time, as the other parent will be working to maintain the family dynamic as well. So at the end of the day, you have a lot of factors at play. Let's take a look at how the DEAL would work in this case.

Describe why it's important to them

Similar to talking to a partner or spouse, your family member is going to want to know why they should change their habits.

Parent: "I've seen a lot of fads come and go; if you want to be vegan, then whatever, but I've been eating this way since before you were born and no one is going to change my mind."

You: "I didn't say anything about being vegan. I'm asking you to replace the processed meats with some alternatives because Grandma died of heart disease and I don't want that to happen to you."

Expect there will be resistance and a feeling of judgment

Parent: "Nonsense, your grandmother's mother ate lots of bacon, smoked two packs a day, and lived to be 89 years old; it's all about moderation and having good genetics. Your grandmother just had a bad heart."

You: "We all make healthy choices based on the information we have at the time. Great-grandma had no idea how bad a lot of that stuff was and got luckier than most. With all the studies that are out now, she very well may have made some different choices."

Answer objections

Parent: "As I said, everything in moderation. Maybe I don't eat the best all the time but no one does, and I've never had an issue with my heart. Last time I checked, you weren't a doctor either."

You: "You're right, I'm not a doctor, and that's why, just like you, I look to doctors and some of these studies to tell me what the best way to live and eat is. A plant-based diet is the only diet that can reverse heart disease, and as the number one killer in the U.S., even if we didn't have a family history, it would be worth trying to prevent. Don't you think it would be worth just making a couple of changes to try it out?"

Leave on a positive note

Parent: "Maybe. I really like bacon, though, and hot dogs, and I don't think these other fake things will be very good."

You: "All I'm asking is to try some of them out, and I'll even go to the store with you. I'm proud you're willing to give it a chance."

You'll notice this exchange wasn't an all-out offensive to get them to go vegan on the spot. This whole situation was just to get the door open for the parent to try some different foods. Here are some additional ideas to help your parents get interested:

Try health first

In the Vomad Study mentioned previously, they asked those surveyed, "What was the main reason for going vegan?" The number one reason was "The Animals" for 80 percent of those that responded, but at number two was for "Health" at 15 percent (Chart 3.1).[3] From those numbers you might be wondering why even bother to talk about health, right? Just show them *Earthlings* or *Dominion*. In the same study, they also broke the respondents down by age. Only 20 percent of those in the study were forty years of age or older, and just 9 percent were fifty or older. Nine percent! This tells me while a majority of younger vegans made the transition for the animals, the same may not be true for older adults who made the change to a plant-based diet.

Chart 3.1: The Main Reason People Go Vegan[3]

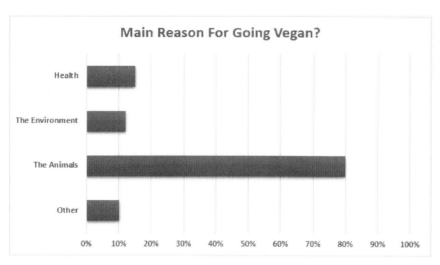

I say this not only as an opinion but from talking to over a hundred parent-age (or older) vegans and asking them why they went vegan. Cancer, heart disease, high cholesterol, you name it, and you will find someone in that 50+ years old group that has gone plant-based to reverse it. Yes, going plant-based is not the same as going vegan, but among the people I talked to it was the stepping stone that allowed them to adopt a cruelty-free lifestyle. Take, for instance, my friend Ed. Ed was diagnosed with cancer. The news was devastating, and like anyone, he weighed the options as to what to do next. After careful consideration and research into the side effects of chemotherapy, he decided what would be best for him would be to adopt a plant-based diet as part of an anti-cancer protocol. In time, his cancer went into remission. After seeing the benefits, Ed continued to eat plant-based and shortly after made the connection to animal suffering. Since he was already eating a typical vegan diet, it was easy to eliminate other animal products as well.

Ed's story is one I've heard over and over: "I had this health issue and changed my diet to reduce the symptoms or cure it. After that, I learned about being vegan and how animals suffer, so I quit using animal products altogether." You can use this model to your advantage. So many conditions have roots stemming from a poor diet: heart disease, cancer, autoimmune diseases, and more. If a parent has an issue or a family history of a disease, use it as a way to open the discussion. Now I wouldn't phrase it as "You need to go vegan before you die from XYZ." Instead, you could say, "I know our family has a history of heart disease, and a lot of people have seen positive benefits from increasing the number of plants in their diet."

Don't make them take your word for it

Have you ever seen the commercial from Rosland Capital telling you to buy gold? Or maybe you've seen an advertisement from AAG about getting a reverse mortgage? They're on YouTube if you haven't. Both of those commercials have something in common: they use celebrities who are older, namely William Devane and Tom Selleck. There's a reason they use these particular people, and that's because their target audience trusts people in their age group more. Sorry, but it's a harsh reality of life to value the opinion and experience of our peers over others. The good news is that if it works for them, it should work for you, and there are literally thousands of stories out there for you to leverage in the same age range as your parents. Two famous people that come right to mind are Dr. Caldwell Esselstyn and Dr. T. Colin Campbell.

Of course, it doesn't need to be someone well-known, as there are undoubtedly people in your community, in your local Facebook, or in Meetup groups. So find someone that your parents might identify with or that might have influence with them. Maybe there is someone vegan at their gym or a neighbor with amazing grass that also happens to be vegan. Ask them to talk to your parents. If you do find someone, it will significantly help your case that being vegan isn't just some trendy thing or a new fad for young people. Show them it's an ageless and global movement for the betterment of all beings.

Speak your parents' language

Depending on your parents' age, you may want to think about how you provide them with information. If your parents are in their sixties like mine, telling them that they need to watch a documentary on Netflix or a video on YouTube is akin to me telling my six-year-old to go watch something on VHS. This is not to generalize older adults or say to it applies to everyone, but let's be realistic, many do not use these technologies, and my Mom is one of them.

My Mom grew up with books, magazines, and newspapers, and quite literally that's still where she gets her information today. She doesn't do online stuff, she doesn't care much for TV unless Survivor is on, and she probably isn't going to change her habits anytime soon. When you are dealing with an older generation, you have to take into consideration the best form of communication. Sending your parents a link to a video on Facebook probably won't have the effect you're looking for, and may even have the opposite.

So think about the best way to reach your parents using a medium that fits within their bubble of communication. For my Mom, it was really just sending her a couple of books. If you find an article online, consider printing it out and giving it to your parent, rather than sending them a link to it, even if it means having to mail it. I know, the shock and horror of actually having to mail something! To the point, if you want to effectively communicate, you have to use the right method for them, not just the easiest or most convenient for you.

It's not a fad, it's the future

In my experience, it's common for the same theme of *it's always been this way* to come up over and over in different forms. The typical "People have always eaten meat, and you're not going to change that" tends to be a favorite response or defense, as it is a mix of the good ol' days and a basic unwillingness to change. As such, it drives a want for you to attack the past, to show how much people were wrong back then, and how much better it is now. However, by doing so, you end up really attacking your parent rather than the topic. For instance, attributing eating animals to smoking, a common thing fifty years ago, may seem like a home run, since most people now realize the dangers of smoking. Doing so, though, is likely to instigate responses that downplay how bad it was, especially if the parent was an ex-smoker who has fond memories of the past that involved smoking. Realistically, it's just not that effective to try and pick a fight about how good or bad things used to be (especially since you probably weren't even alive then), so don't get sucked into it.

Instead, paint a picture of the future. You can say "That may have been the case in the past, but the future is meat-free." You have all the resources in the world to show that being vegan isn't just some fad but that it's an international trend that is gaining momentum quickly. As stated before, the percent of people that are adopting a vegan lifestyle is increasing rapidly, restaurants are introducing menu changes every day, and consumer products are increasingly labeling their products as vegan. These types of significant changes are not the kind you see for a fad. Large companies may put out some products to meet a current market trend or advertise to a specific market to increase profits. However, what large companies don't do for a fad is rapidly acquire whole companies, such as the purchase of Daiya foods by Japanese-owned Otsuka, or make expensive investments into companies like Beyond Meat, as Bill Gates and Tyson Farms have done. So when you are out and about with your parents, be sure to point out that T.G.I. Friday's has the Beyond Meat burger now, and that Mellow Mushroom has vegan pizza. By doing so, you can show to them that it's a global trend.

Don't rush it

Lastly, my recommendation would be to plant small seeds and don't rush the process. Push small changes like having your parents try plant-milks or vegan ice cream that get them interested instead of negative comments about their current food choices. Allow them to discover for themselves why so many people are making the switch to plant-based foods, and be a resource for questions rather than a bearer of bad news.

YOUR KIDS

Your children should be no problem, right? They are under your roof so it's "Go vegan or you're grounded!" The sad truth is that this really does kind of work, at least at home. As a parent you do have a large degree of control over meals and shopping for food, so, by all means, you can set the tone at home. However, when your child walks out the door, they are sure to be bombarded with a barrage of advertising, misinformation, peer-pressure, and possibly social rejection. In short, they will face a lot, and if you want your kids to be more than just plant-based at home, it's going to take more than "Do as I say."

The good news? Kids are fantastic, and they are generally very in tune with their emotions. They are much more likely to feel empathy for others and, depending on their age, they probably have limited exposure to the lengthy ad campaigns that have done so much damage to past generations, like "Got Milk?" and "Where's the Beef?" Knowing that, use their empathetic nature to make a case for the animals, and use age-appropriate language or media to describe to them the importance of reducing animal suffering. Let's check out that DEAL acronym again.

Describe why it's important to them

Unlike your parents, your kids probably don't have a slew of health issues; thus, your focus should really revolve around animal suffering and the environment. Kids naturally care about others and the world around them, so let them know the reality of how their actions impact other beings and the Earth.

You: "I want you to know that I have decided to give up eating and buying animal products because of how much suffering it causes and how bad it is for the earth."

Them: "Does that mean we can't have pizza or hotdogs anymore?"

You: "We can still have those things, but we are just going to get ones that are made from plants instead. However, you are free to make your own choices outside of the house."

Expect there will be resistance and a feeling of judgment

Them: "But I like those things, and didn't you used to eat all that stuff when you were a kid?"

You: "Yes, I did, but I also didn't know the impact I was having or that I had another choice. I know now that eating that stuff was unhealthy and hurt a lot of animals."

Answer objections

Them: "But all my friends eat that kind of stuff; they are going to think I'm weird if I'm just eating tofu."

You: "Well, do all your friends eat the same thing, or do they each have certain foods they don't eat?"

Them: "I guess I have a friend that doesn't eat olives…"

You: "There you go. Everyone makes different choices concerning what foods they eat, and there's nothing weird about it."

Leave on a positive note

You: "You are free to make your own choices outside the house, but I want you to be informed as to how they make those hot dogs and that pizza. I know you are smart and will make the best decision for you."

Again, a simple conversation, but one that makes a case for veganism in a positive and reinforcing manner. Obviously, if your child is young, you don't want to sit them down and flood them with images and videos of slaughterhouses, so you have to make the conversation age appropriate. However, I would urge that you do your best to convey the suffering of the animals. Make the case so that your child knows that it really is life or death for them and that their pain isn't some far-off fantasy, but it's happening every day around the world, and likely in their hometown. Give them a real reason to go vegan that they can hold on to and believe in.

Isn't this brainwashing?

You might be saying to yourself, "Now wait just a minute, isn't this wrong force feeding my child my vegan beliefs, and won't everyone call me a bad parent for doing this?" I know there are many parents who probably never even had this thought cross their mind, but there are lots, including myself, that had to struggle with this question for a while, especially if they are new to being vegan. When my wife and I first went vegan many years ago, we struggled with whether or not we should make our infant daughter vegan as well. That sounds rather silly, knowing everything I know now, but back in 2012, we were the only vegans we knew. There weren't as many resources then as there are now for new vegans, and we had a lot of pressure from family, friends, and our pediatrician to keep her on an omni diet. So it honestly took us a while before we felt comfortable with making the jump for her, but ultimately we made that decision.

As part of that process, I think my wife and I both had some hesitation because we were essentially making a choice that would affect her every day. While other kids went to McDonald's for happy meals, she would go to the local vegan restaurant instead. At birthday parties, she would have to bring her own treats, while all the other kids ate birthday cake and pizza. That stuff weighed on us, but looking back now I wish we had made the decision sooner. Those things that seemed like a big deal were actually not, and she has always had a good time at parties, including her own vegan parties, with lots of friends happy to share in her vegan cake and food.

As for the brainwashing part, we quickly learned and took the stance that, yes, we were making the decision for her, but the real brainwashing was done by the industries themselves that target children in the first place. That is to say, if your children grew up in the wild with no one else, you can guess they would likely not be eating various meat products, but would instead be consuming a diet rich in fruits, vegetables, nuts, and roots—no different than most similar primates. So realize that our society has been set up to push these products and make you feel as if you are denying them something, or that they are missing out by not eating the meat and dairy industries products. You should never feel that you are forcing your beliefs on your children, but instead protecting them from a lifetime of health issues, as well as protecting the animals who would be their faceless victims. It is, in essence, a heroic and remarkable act of compassion to push back against a society that demonizes you for not allowing the meat and dairy industry to make choices for your children.

Don't forget the environment

I think it's fair to say that most parents remember talking about the environment in school and how important it was to be a good steward for the environment. When I was in school, the big push was to "Reduce, Reuse, and Recycle." To this day I still use that little phrase, and as a kid, I can remember it being a big deal. The underlying point being that kids actually do care about the environment. If you are a new vegan and you haven't made the connection between reduced consumption of animal products and the environment yet, there are many documentaries and articles out there for you to do so.

We will go into some objections later in this book as to exactly how the environment is affected, but on the kid level, you don't have to dive into the fine details. Instead, just hit the highlights: agriculture has a significant impact on our climate, and it's the largest producer of greenhouse gases in the world; it has resulted in millions of acres of forests being cleared to make room for pasture and our oceans being depleted of marine life by reckless fishing practices.[4,5,6] If age-appropriate, you can show them videos of the methods, such as videos of commercial fishing vessels in action. If they are very young, you can explain the practices in simpler terms, show them kid-friendly videos (such as Sesame Street), or read to them classics like the Dr. Seuss' *The Lorax*—one of my daughter's favorite books.

Making the animal connection

Books and videos are great, but they only go so far. If you want to have a significant impact, then allow your children to meet the animals who are the victims of industry violence. If you can, take them to an animal

61

sanctuary and let them experience firsthand the life that must be lost to produce the products in the supermarket. At a sanctuary, they will be able to not only see the animals in their natural and free environment but also meet their caretakers who actively resist against such a violent system. There you can ask real questions to your kids, like, "Do you think it's okay for someone to hurt these animals?" It's as real of a situation as you can get, with the actual victim standing in front of them. I would be willing to bet that it will have a lasting impact and hopefully a positive one as well.

Unsupportive family

As important as it is to convince your children to go vegan, it's almost as essential to create an environment where they will not be pressured by other family members to eat or use animal products. If your children are older, it could be as easy as prepping them to deal with situations where other family members might offer them animal products. For younger children, if you have an unsupportive family member, it can be… frustrating is probably the nicest way to put it, because they see you as depriving your child of the wonderful things they had as children. In this case, you will have to either set clear boundaries that it is unacceptable to feed your young children animal products, or, in extreme circumstances, you may have to restrict them from unsupervised interaction. I actually had to do this with a family member who was purposely giving my child dairy because she was worried that a life experience would be missed, with no regard for the life that had to produce that product.

In the case of an unsupportive spouse, especially if you are separated, the situation can be more than difficult. You can't control the other parent's access to your child, and no judge would probably ever agree to make the other parent feed your child a plant-based diet. Again, if the child is older, you can help them to understand why animal products are so harmful, but if they are young, there's not much you can do to control the situation. What you can do is do your best by trying to convince the other parent using the techniques in this book, promoting how much better your child looks and feels when they are eating plant-based foods, and small things like sending your child's favorite recipes with them to the other parent's house. Try to be creative on how to influence the other parent. If they won't budge, then at least be proud that your child is eating plant-based foods at least while they are with you, and that you are doing everything you can to make the best of the situation.

Be the example

Most important of all, if you want your kids to pursue a life of compassion, you have to set the example, and this applies to all your friends and family as well! While you probably think I'm talking about just being vegan, I'm actually talking about being the kind of person that makes others want to be vegan too. If you are the kind of person that continually engages in heated confrontations, either in person or online, your child is probably going to be put off. If you show being vegan means being angry at everyone else, no one is going to want any part of that lifestyle. Is it tempting to shame that person in the checkout line next to you with a cart full of meat products, talking to their spouse about how their diabetes is causing problems today? You bet! How I have wanted to jump all over someone and tell them, "Hey, it's your food choices that are the issue!" Don't do it.

Not only does that go against what we talked about in Chapter 2, it just shows your child that being vegan means being confrontational, and that's not what you want. Instead, show how your choices impact others and impact the world around you. Show them that by buying more fruit and vegetables you use less plastic and Styrofoam that frequently accompanies meat purchases, like meat trays. Show them how amazing your food can be with no meat products, or how exciting it is to try a whole bunch of new plant-milks.

Last, let your child know just how much they are not missing out on. Phrases like, "You're so lucky to have meals like this vegan mac and cheese; it's way better than I had growing up," can go a long way to show them they are not being deprived, but being rewarded for their choice. In short, make living a vegan lifestyle a positive and attractive option, not just one that they have to or should do.

YOUR FRIENDS (OR SIBLINGS/CLOSE FAMILY)

Hopefully, you have some friends left after going vegan! I've actually gained a lot of new friends through vegan meetups and pot-lucks. Personally, I can say I never lost any friends after switching my diet, and I would expect most people don't if they were half-decent friends to begin with. Nonetheless, you might actually risk some friendships as you attempt to get them to change their habits as well. So where do you start? Do you just go up and say, "Hey, I think you should go vegan; look how much I love it!" It can be a little intimidating for sure, especially since you don't want to ruin a friendship trying to force the other person to do something they don't want to do. Thus, just like we have been talking about so far, you want to make sure it doesn't become a battle of wills or an argument, but an attractive concept that makes them want to make that change.

So how can you influence your friends to go vegan, but not make it an awkward or uncomfortable situation? As usual, use the DEAL method.

Describe why it's important to them
Them: "Man, I am feeling really worn out today; you ever feel like that?"

You: "Oh yeah, I used to all the time, especially after a big meal, but since I've been eating a lot more fruits and veggies, it doesn't happen as often."

Expect there will be resistance and a feeling of judgment
Them: "Oh, here we go, so vegans never get tired then, right?"

You: "Hey, you asked me. I just don't get that 'heavy' feeling anymore like I used to after eating animal products, so a big salad and I'm ready to go."

Answer objections
Them: "Ugh, that sounds terrible. You don't see cheetahs or other high-energy animals eating grass... I think I need a burger or something."

You: "Pretty sure when cheetahs finish their meal they end up lying around for hours digesting, and the animals they are chasing are just as fast or faster. Deer, for instance, eat nothing but plants and have tons of energy. That's me, I'm like a gazelle!"

Leave on a positive note

Them: "Haha, okay, I guess, but who wants to eat salad?"

You: "Hey, I will bring you something special tomorrow that will blow your taste buds away, and you'll probably feel better too."

It's just that easy to change someone's habits without having to resort to guilt or force. When the friend said that they were "tired" the conversation didn't turn into, "You wouldn't be so tired if you didn't pay someone to kill animals and eat their bodies, you horrible person." Okay, a bit of overkill again, but that's really what some people do, and it never works. What did happen was the conversation revolved around plants giving you energy and ended with an offer to help the friend with a gift. That's the kind of exchange you want, and that makes a positive impact, one that isn't a battle of wills and wits, but friends being friends and caring about each other.

Eating out

Most of us spend a lot of time eating out with two types of people: our family and our friends. When you do go out to eat with your friends, it's an opportunity for you to either show how easy and great it is to be vegan or how horrible and difficult it is to be vegan. I think you may already know what I'm talking about. Now, granted, sometimes you will end up at a place that really does make it as difficult as humanly possible to eat plant-based foods. Applebee's comes to mind as a restaurant that seems to deliberately sabotage its menu with meat products in every dish (hint, hint, Applebee's, add more options!).

If you can choose the restaurant, try to pick one that provides you the opportunity to show your friend how great plant-based foods can be. T.G.I. Friday's comes to my mind immediately, if only because I have had the chance to share many Beyond Burgers with my curious friends.

When we go, I make it a big deal, and I make it a special "vegans" only deal. I'll say, "Yeah, let's go to T.G.I. Friday's. They have this amazing veggie burger made just for vegans." When the waiter brings it out, I'll make it a point to say how good it looks and groan over how good it tastes, even though I've had it many times before. The point is, I go out of my way to talk it up, versus what you might see others do, trying to shame the other person eating a meat-based meal—a sure way to not get invited back to lunch again and being labeled "that angry vegan."

Social media

I have no doubt that your friends are probably on social media as well; they probably like your Facebook posts and follow your tweets. However, if you have been vegan for a while and you make it a point to post endless animal rights and pro-vegan posts, you might be looking around wondering where all your friends went. I can tell you that I am whole-heartedly guilty of this. When I first went vegan, I thought that this is something that everyone needed to hear about. *If I just post some of these videos and pictures, people will really take note, and maybe some will change their habits.* How many of my friends do you think were like, "Wow, this is awful; I need to make a change"? If your answer was anything more than a big fat zero, then you have as much faith as I had going in. I really did feel that social media could be a platform for change, and it can, but not like that. The more you post facts on veganism, or videos that depict violence towards animals, the more you will find your friends disappearing or clicking the dreaded unfollow button.

No one finds this more frustrating than me, because there are some fantastic resources out there that are truly powerful. Gary Yourofsky's "Best Speech You Will Ever Hear" comes to mind; however, people will not give it the time of day unless they are in the right mindset to do so. So what can you do? The key is super simple. Wash your posts of anything vegan and place the focus on what's most important to your friends: you! Instead of posts demanding your friends to eat less meat, post pictures of your amazing dinner with the recipe, and don't say a word about it being vegan. Rather than trying to show how horrible leather belts are with graphic pictures, show off your new cork belt and post how durable and amazing it is. Rather than posting slaughterhouse videos, post videos of how you make your favorite plant-based snacks—kale chips, for instance, are becoming very popular and easy to make. I posted a video of how to make hot sauce on my Facebook timeline, and people loved it. It's that famous phrase "You catch more flies with agave than vinegar." Okay, I added agave, but you get the point, and this way you will be able to plant the same seeds with a hope for making an impact, instead of sending your friends running from an onslaught of off-putting posts.

Now you might be thinking, "Now wait a minute, AJ, why should I sugarcoat reality? They should be forced to see the horrible things they are doing to animals, and I need to be their voice." If you had one chance to make an impact to a stranger, I would agree with you, and that's a technique that is employed by various organizations, like Anonymous for the Voiceless, which I'll talk about later. However, if you continuously bombard your friends with negative and violent media, they will likely start considering why they are friends with you at all. So do yourself and your friends a favor, and take it easy on them. You have the advantage of applying positive pressure over time, so don't be in a rush to push the issue. Allow them to make the change on their own terms, just like you probably did, and they will not only still be your friend in the end, but thank you for not being that typical vegan.

That friend

What about "that friend," that instead of getting annoyed about you being vegan, goes on the offensive. That friend that constantly goes out of their way to post offensive pictures on your social media or makes jokes at your expense each time you meet up. I don't want to say that this is the norm, because I think most friends jest a bit but also have good boundaries. However, it isn't uncommon to see someone who is being—to say the least—bullied by their so-called friends on their choice to go vegan. If this is you and you have someone in your life like this, first know that you are certainly not the only one, and second, the vast amount of anti-vegan propaganda out there is usually the source of much of it.

I would never tell anyone to put up with such treatment and be the subject of constant harassment. However, I will say that some jesting is not uncommon and as ugly as some of the content may be, especially when it comes to the violence inflicted by industry, it may be worth taking it with a grain of salt. That is to say, your friend probably has no idea how offensive some of the comments can be, and you can defuse the situation and salvage the friendship with some serious conversation. I know this is probably a "well, duh" comment for some, but you would be surprised to see how often it happens and how often others are at a loss for what to do about it.

Whether it's a friend, spouse, coworker, or whoever is doing the harassment, give them the benefit of the doubt that they don't know how much negativity they are injecting with their comments. In a private and appropriate moment, use the DEAL strategy to try to defuse the situation. If you do all of that and the harassment continues, it would be fair to examine whether the friendship is worth it.

Being a friend first and vegan second

I once saw a post online of a person that said, "I can't take the carnism anymore, getting rid of all my friends and replacing them with other vegans, vegan friend me please!" You may literally get to the point you want to ditch your friends for other likeminded friends; it's a natural and a normal thing. It is no doubt difficult being a vegan, knowing the pain and suffering the animals are enduring, and, for instance, then going to dinner with two non-vegan friends who casually eat the remains of those animals without a care in the world. In such a moment, take heed to remember that your friends are a product of long-standing culture and unless they are a new friend, they are probably still adapting to your change from meat-eater to vegan.

So take a deep breath at times and remember that you, too—and I'm guessing for most of us—had to undergo a transformation that likely took months or maybe years. Every conversation and every meal does not, and should not, be a conversation that leads back to being vegan. Yes, use all the means available for you to make a case for the animals and for a cruelty-free life, but allow room for your friends to grow as well. If every conversation ends up in a battle over why they aren't vegan yet, there won't be many conversations to follow, because your friends will run for the hills when they see you!

YOUR COWORKERS

If you're working full-time, you probably spend a lot more time with your coworkers than just about anyone else. Most days I spend upwards of nine hours with my coworkers and about four with my family (if you subtract out the time we are sleeping). With so much time together, most of my coworkers and former coworkers are also some of my closest friends. I'm sure many of you have similar relationships with your coworkers. You get to hear a lot about their lives, pets, health issues, and even weird things like how they dumped an entire bottle of peppermint oil in their air conditioner trying to deter mice, but ended up turning their house into a candy factory with a smell so thick they had to call in an emergency HVAC team. True story, and very kind to mice for a guy that's not even vegan.

Thus, what you have is tremendous opportunity to turn your workplace from carnivore city into a plant-based wonderland. Every day, you have the chance to consistently make a case for being vegan, not only by being a model of good health and compassion but sharing your knowledge and culinary skills. Just like with all the previous examples, I use the same DEAL method at my work and slowly but surely being vegan wasn't just some weird hippie thing, but a "Yeah, my coworker is vegan, and he really likes it. "

Here's a sample of a discussion I had in my office:

Describe why it's important to them

Them: "That is a huge container of soup; how on Earth can you always eat so much and stay so thin!"

You: "Well, because it's just vegetables and beans it really doesn't have that many calories."

Expect there will be resistance and a feeling of judgment

Them: "I guess; seems like it would be a lot easier to just eat a healthy well-balanced lunch instead, like a turkey sandwich."

You: "I don't know how that could be considered well-balanced without any fiber or the nutrition that comes with lots of veggies and beans."

Answer objections

Them: "Well, it's more filling because the turkey is all protein and it has all the nutrition I need."

You: "Turkey may have protein, but that's only because the turkey got its protein and nutrition from plants first. Why eat second-hand protein loaded with cholesterol and saturated fat, when the beans in my soup give the same amount but without all the bad stuff?"

Leave on a positive note

Them: "Hmm, I guess I never really thought about them getting all there protein from plants."

You: "Yeah, and you end up eating all that cholesterol too. Do you want the recipe for this soup?"

This scenario plays out at my work all the time, and to be honest, it seems like I am always bringing stuff in for others to try. A big point here, before moving on, is that nowhere in that conversation did the word "vegan" come up. That's not to say that vegan is a bad word, but it has a tendency to become more than just a statement. For instance, if you were to say "I would never eat a turkey sandwich because I'm vegan, and you should be vegan too," you can see how that comes off. It's basically saying, "I'm better than you, and you should be like me." So try to keep that term at bay and if others say that, "Oh, this is our office vegan," downplay it a bit, so it doesn't come off as a title that owns you. Similarly, if your coworker says, "We need to find a different lunch spot because you are vegan," then you might interject and say, "Hey, I'm just trying to eat the best food for me." That instantly changes the vibe from your coworkers accommodating your special diet to making something work for everyone because everyone has different tastes.

Going to lunch/potlucks

Here where I live, on the Emerald Coast, there is a local Mexican-style restaurant chain called Burrito Del Sol. Burrito Del Sol has grown quite a bit since I first started going there in 2015 from one small restaurant to two, with a significant expansion at their main site. It's a very hip hangout that combines a Mexican restaurant with the beachy vibe that is ever-present here. The menu isn't huge, and it's not vegan, but it has something that is rare to find, especially around this area. It has tempeh. Not just any tempeh, mind you, but the best tempeh you've probably ever had in your life. It's gingery, sweet, smoky, and it changes everything about what you thought tempeh could be. No, really, it's incredible!

Besides being my favorite tempeh and one of the best burritos ever, Burrito Del Sol has served a different purpose as my way of introducing friends and coworkers to something they've probably never tried before, let alone heard of. Over the course of several lunches, what started as a casual interest into what I was eating, with statements like, "Fermented soybeans, that sounds nasty," quickly ended in, "We'll all have the tempeh please." How amazing is that? I didn't have to throw down facts about how meat is destroying the environment or shame them into giving up meat in their meals. They, being my three coworkers that I usually go to lunch with, all took turns trying this new and intriguing thing I was eating and decided that it was actually better than the other choices.

Now clearly that is a testament to Burrito Del Sol for having awesome tempeh, but it was also my expressed enjoyment of the tempeh and talking it up that piqued their interest. You can do the same with your local restaurants as well. If you know a spot that has something really exceptional or unique, get your coworkers to go and talk it up. Maybe you know a Chinese place that has amazing tofu stir-fry or a place with phenomenal pho. Whatever the dish, get it, talk it up, and offer some to your coworkers so they can see that compassionate and healthy choices are every bit as good, or better, than animal-based choices.

If you're not the type to go out for lunch or your workplace isn't conducive to that, no problem; bring some of your favorite foods to them. Potlucks are the perfect place to showcase many of the fantastic recipes that are out there, and just by the nature of a potluck, others are likely to be more adventurous. Two of my all-time favorite potluck recipes are taco soup and black bean brownies, both easy to find on Google. The taco soup recipe actually garnered the comment, "I thought you didn't eat meat," in response to my coworker finding a "meat" looking thing in the soup; it was actually Beyond Beef crumble, and he was completely fooled by it. The black bean brownie recipe is equally as sneaky, as you can't taste the beans at all, and they are really, really good. The end result of the potlucks? "Hey, when are you bringing in some more of those brownies?" It's an excellent opportunity to show how plant-based eating isn't some weird thing or about only eating salads, and you definitely won't get any typical anti-vegan arguments as your coworkers are stuffing their faces.

Coffee

What workplace doesn't have coffee? I love coffee, and thankfully, as I write this, Dr. Gregor hasn't put out any videos on his website, nutritionfacts.org, saying not to drink it. More than just my love for coffee, I wanted to include it here because it's such an easy way to showcase the transition away from dairy and toward the adoption of plant-milks. What better way than to stock the workplace fridge with plant-based milks and creamers? Who could resist the desire to try out hazelnut milk or coconut creamer in their coffee, especially when it's right there in the fridge and the alternative is that old powdered creamer that's been sitting on the counter for two or three years? This is probably the easiest thing in the world to lure your coworkers to the dark side, and have them rave about how good it is. Then when they do confess their new found love for plant milk, you have the perfect opportunity to throw in all the other things they can put it in, from cereal to baking.

Health topics

This may depend on where you work and the age group of people you work with, but generally speaking, it seems like the issue of health arises a lot in the workplace. If someone, or someone in their family, is having health issues, it's an excellent opportunity to bring up the benefits of a plant-based diet. For instance, one of my coworkers was very concerned about breast cancer. Although she's never had it, she was worried about it due to a long family history of the disease, and she took lengthy steps to determine her risk, including doing BRCA1/2 gene testing 15 years before it's recommended to have done. What an opportunity it was to be able to suggest to her a large amount of vegan-based foods she could consume to reduce her cancer risk, like soy and flax seed.

Similarly, another coworker had high cholesterol and was worried about developing heart disease later in life. How excited he was to hear that a plant-based diet is the only diet ever proven to reverse heart disease.[7] After that discussion, he started making changes to include a lot more plant-based foods in his diet. Lots of health topics seem to come up often, so don't miss your chance to throw out some suggestions for your coworkers to research on their own.

Keep *what's its* on your desk

People often come by my desk at work, and every time they do, they, intentionally or not, look at all the stuff I have laying around and posted up. Knowing that my coworkers simply cannot resist asking "What is this?" to something new or interesting, I purposely leave a variety of things around that either spark a conversation or draw interest. Food is an obvious and easy thing to have. It's not uncommon for there to be a large bag of homemade kale chips sitting on my desk, made from kale I grow year round in my garden. Yes, I like kale chips, but they are really there for others to try so they can get interested in new foods, especially since the "cheese" is vegan too. Also, because the cheese is made from nutritional yeast, it makes a great introduction to something most non-vegans have never heard of.

Some other things I try to keep around are articles or books about plant-based eating or health. For instance, I always keep a copy of *Shred It!* by Robert Cheeke, because it always seems that someone is trying to lose weight or start going back to the gym. Since I'm in pretty fair shape, I often get asked that most annoying of questions, "Where do you get your protein?" To which I can quickly respond that I get plenty of protein, and so does Robert Cheeke, who is not only vegan but also a two-time natural body-building champion, and he recommends eating a lower protein diet packed with nutrition. I have been fortunate enough to meet Robert, and he is the real deal, as well as an awesome guy that really cares about people's fitness and health.

The end point is that you can keep all kinds of *what's its* around, and they will help you to share being vegan without having to engage others or be awkward about it. Your coworkers will be able to come to you interested in what you have on their own time, without it feeling like you are trying to push something on them. So keep some vegan chocolate on your desk or some gelatin-free gummies. Show how good, and easy, it is to leave out the cruelty.

EVERYONE YOU MEET

Family and friends are great, but what if you want to take on the whole world? If vegan activism gets you excited and you can't wait to get out there and make a difference, you're definitely not alone. For decades PETA has staged hundreds of demonstrations, and many new activist groups are taking root, like Anonymous for the Voiceless, the Save Movement, and Direct Action Everywhere (DXE). Many have taken up the challenge to fight the meat and dairy industry, and while some change minds on a daily basis, others foster resistance and anger towards vegans instead.

Just this month it was announced in the news that a group of alleged vegans made bomb threats and vandalized a butcher shop in the town of Ashford in Kent, England. Online, the act drew praise from vegan groups who condemned the shop and were glad to see fellow vegans taking a stand for the animals. So what happened? Did the shop close? Did they change their business to a vegan butcher shop? No, instead hundreds of people came to the rescue of the "poor" small business owner who was being harassed by angry protestors. The actions of the protestors resulted in the business receiving almost four-hundred 5-Star reviews in a matter of days and lots of new customers, eager to show their support for their local business. Some of the comments on their Facebook page sum up the actions perfectly:

"It's almost funny how their method of stopping 'cruelty and violence,' is by using cruelty and violence."

"We live a forty-minute drive from this butcher but will take the time to drive there from now on to support this family business. I feel disgusted by those extremists and want to support you in any way."

Clearly, this is failed activism. Now I don't expect many of you will be calling in bomb threats, but the point should be clear that if you do desire to make a change in the public arena, there is a right way and a wrong way to do it. Let's take a quick look at more of what not to do.

The wrong way

If I gave you the keyboard, you could probably write this part yourself. You already know that people who are aggressive, agitated, and confrontational are unlikely to have any kind of positive impact; and yet how quickly we tend to fall into that mentality when defending veganism to others. A perfect example is to ask someone, "Why do you eat meat when you know animals are suffering?" and have them reply, "Well, that's terrible, but I don't really care that much." How does that make you feel? Are you ready to fight it out now? I can tell you I for sure am! I'm thinking, "You don't care?" as I'm rolling up my sleeves. It's the natural reaction to want to defend another who is suffering, and it's easy to lose sight of the end goal. The reality is, just being out in public spreading a message will tend to draw confrontational people, and your ability to defuse that will directly impact your influence on the other person's perception of vegans. If someone tries to push your buttons and you react in retaliation, others around will either become disinterested or, worse, come to the other person's defense.

The language you use could also hurt your ability to persuade others from going vegan, and there are four words I suggest you never use: rape, murder, slavery, and the Holocaust. Are animals *raped* on factory farms? There is a strong case to use that word to describe the process, but you likely do so at your own detriment. While forced impregnation is a horrible practice and comparing it to what we as a culture have defined as *rape* makes sense, it falls short of the violence and emotional damage that the word implies. In using that word, you risk a possible strong and emotional reaction in reply from anyone that has been assaulted or knows someone who has. *Murder* falls in the same circumstance; again, you risk opening underlying trauma, and the discussion will quickly depart from anything about veganism.

Any references to slavery should be avoided as well, as it is a topic that is sure to create a debate over its use taking away from the suffering of so many who have and continue to endure such treatment around the world. I have personally heard slavery used many times and visually seen it as memes on vegan sites. Each time, you can see the comment section ignite over such a comparison, and it's not really to anyone's benefit to use a term which has such a tragic history. It's better to instead use more fitting terms like incarceration or imprisonment.

Lastly, I would recommend not making any reference to the Holocaust, Nazis, or the suffering of the Jewish people under their regime. Media and culture love to use the images and horror of Nazi Germany to showcase evil actions; however, not only is it highly offensive, it's often ineffective as well, since such a comparison has been so overused it has all but lost any impact. There are more examples that are inappropriate, too many to list here, so instead, I would recommend just taking a second to think before you speak in a public forum. Think about what others might find offensive or lead off topic, because if your message falls into heated cultural or social issues, it could quickly spiral into a debate you don't want to have.

Increasing awareness

So what can you do? Instead of having the goal in mind to change someone's mind on the spot, just make it your goal to increase awareness and showcase a positive image. If you make it your goal to raise awareness, then you will be much more likely to draw in interest than you would be when trying to confront someone and change their habits on the spot. While there is no one way to do something, a group I already mentioned—Anonymous for the Voiceless—gets a lot of things right. If you have ever been to one of their Cube of Truth demonstrations, you'll notice that no one is staring you down or running up to confront you. The demonstrators wear masks that take the person out of the equation and allow the viewer to focus on the animal footage. If someone shows interest, there are other activists nearby to answer questions and provide resources if they would like to know more. In short, the whole setup is there to share the message, increase awareness, and do so in a manner that doesn't intimidate. Doesn't sound like much, but it is a significant departure from the traditional protest method.

Do I expect you to buy a mask and run down to join your local cube? I would love it and would hop in any cube with you, but I know it's not for everyone. However, if you do engage in public activism, whether online or in-person, I think it's a great idea to keep in mind how you approach others and interact with them. Instead of yelling and condemning someone at the store for buying a package of meat, you might mention that you saw a video that changed your mind and hand them a card with the website on it. Instead of demanding that the local restaurant serve vegan options, you might ask the owner if they have ever considered adding various fake meats to their menu and give them a print out of some Gardein products. You can do all kinds of public activism without being the angry vegan most have in mind, and you can do so by focusing on increasing awareness rather than trying to force the issue.

Here is a great example using our favorite DEAL method of a real conversation I had about a circus in my town:

Describe why it's important to them

Them: "Don't you vegans have something better to do than protest this local circus?"

You: "Actually, I'm surprised that there aren't more people here. I just recently learned that this circus has been cited with multiple violations by the USDA. Were you aware they had been charged with animal abuse?"

Expect there will be resistance and a feeling of judgment

Them: "Look, I bring my kids here every year, and I've never seen any abuse. It's a family friendly show, and I'd appreciate it if you would stop harassing people."

You: "I'm sorry if you feel like its harassment, but we are simply raising awareness on this issue."

Answer objections

Them: "If there were serious concerns, the USDA would shut down the circus, so I'm not buying it."

You: "I actually have a printed list of USDA citations right here. What do you think of all these violations?"

Leave on a positive note

Them: "Hmm, well I guess that's not a good thing, but we already got tickets so we are still going to go."

You: "I understand. I would ask that you please consider what kind of treatment would motivate these animals to perform the tricks they do and if you do see any signs of abuse, please let us know so we can alert the authorities. Thanks for listening."

Never forget that activism is a long game strategy. It's less about trying to win someone over today as it is just getting the conversation started. So use that mindset when you engage with others; just get the conversation started and let them find some of the truths for themselves.

Protesting

"I know what we can do, we can protest!" Protesting or holding public events to gain attention for animal rights have been mainstays for decades. As I'm writing this book, several large marches in NYC and London have just concluded, with thousands in attendance. While protesting can be an effective tool, it can also be misused and actually hurt your cause. A recent study found that although extreme protests—ones that involve things like violence, vandalism, and blocking traffic—gain more media attention, they actually result in less support for the cause.[8] It seems counter-intuitive that you could get more attention yet less support, but the key lies in the view of the bystander. Protests that are extreme, as opposed to moderate, cause bystanders to disassociate themselves with the protestors, or, in short, they can't relate with them. If you see images of protesters breaking windows or standing in the road, those not in the movement are more likely to say, "I'm not like them." Right there you lose the whole purpose of the protest.

The big take away is that whatever method you chose to bring attention to your cause, you should stop to consider the moderate bystander. You should ask, "How will this look to them? How will they see my actions? Can they relate to our cause?" Nonviolence, like marches and events, convey moderation and help establish a connection to the average person. More so, if you can include common identifiable symbols in your march, such as patriotic flags or popular culture references, the more likely you are to make the connection to the other person that "You are like us, and you can identify with our cause."

For the same circus mentioned earlier, I led a demonstration to raise awareness for the animals and to urge the local government to consider inviting an animal-free circus next year. We had U.S. flags visible during the event, and I encouraged everyone to wear local sports team shirts and hats so that we would be more identifiable to the community. One more thing, I never used the word *protest* because it has such negative and extremist connotations. So when people asked "Why are you protesting," my response was always "I'm not protesting, I'm raising awareness."

Technology as a global platform

We have talked a lot about social media, and to be honest, I could write a whole section about it, but I think that is unnecessary. Just like we have talked about not getting into arguments and being compassionate, the same is going to apply online as well. Do people go online to troll and get a rise out of you? You bet. However, the more you personify the angry vegan image, the more people will believe that being vegan isn't for them. Be cool. Show everyone that being vegan is more than getting into arguments online. If someone posts pictures of violence, post photos of vegan food or plants. It sounds dumb, I'm sure, but you're better off doing just about anything other than feeding the trolls. The same goes with your friends. If they post things that you find offensive, either look for something positive in the post or ignore it. You might think that you have to be a social vegan warrior 24/7 and everyone will cheer for you, but you'll probably just upset your friends and followers, and then they will be gone along with your chance to change their minds. Instead, make posts and send tweets that are positive, smart, and tactical.

Lastly, let's talk about passive activism. While documentaries consti-tute a significant source of information, and thousands of people have decided to go vegan from watching them, they are not the only source of passive media. I say passive because after making a creation—a book or video, for instance—you no longer have to do the work during each interaction; it, instead, does the job for you. For as many people as I have met that went vegan from watching *Forks over Knives* or *What the Health*, there seem to be just as many that made the switch from only watching videos on YouTube like Gary Yourofsky's speech and "Dairy is Scary" by Erin Janus. Both of these have a significant thing in common: they were made by people just like you and I. You too can make these kinds of powerful videos just as well as the next person; Mic the Vegan even has free instruction on how to do that on his website, MicThe-Vegan.com. You can write a blog or ebook with the power to convince hundreds or thousands of people to go vegan. So don't think that you are just limited to personal interactions, be it online or in person. There is a whole world out there that you can influence if you so choose to do so!

YOU CAN ONLY DO SO MUCH—
IT'S A PERSONAL CHANGE

So you've tried the DEAL method, asked questions, patiently answered question after question, and still, the other person won't give up the animal products... what now? Habits are addicting and a lifetime of consuming animal products is hard to overcome for many. Not only are they cheaper than they should be, thanks to government subsidies, but the meat and dairy industries aren't going down without a fight, much like big tobacco still continues to sell its products even in the face of overwhelming medical recommendations and continued media pressure against smoking. If you remember back to the very beginning of this book, I mentioned something that was crucial to changing someone's behavior: they have to *want* to change. While you can certainly put the odds in your favor, the reality is that they may never make the change to a plant-based lifestyle, or maybe you aren't the right person to get them to change. Perhaps they don't like your personality or the way you dress, and that's enough to put them off from talking about vegan topics with you. It happens.

What you can do is, just like I also mentioned, keep that long game in mind. Don't give up and don't think that just because you didn't win the fight today that you are not winning the war. Back to that Vomad study on what made people decide to go vegan, while 37 percent went vegan due to friends and family, that means a good majority of the rest found their way to enlightenment through other means. That is to say, some just have to find their own way and walk their own path. That certainly doesn't mean that everything we just talked about is out the window, though. While it may have been that Netflix documentary that was the tipping point for someone, you may have aided in the process without even knowing it by posting a link on social media. Bottom line, the seeds you sow may grow when you least expect it, and you may not even know you helped to plant the garden around you. Never give up!

CHAPTER 4
DIFFERENT TYPES OF PEOPLE

ONE THING I find useful when talking to people, whether old friends or new, is to try to get an idea of what kind of category they fall into so I can tailor my responses to better gain interest, prepare for their unique objections, and most importantly, to find common ground. This probably sounds lame, and a bit presumptuous to put a label on others, but it's no different from our discussion on protesting. You want to show that both you and your friend have similar interests and are in the same group of common individuals or tribe. This is critically important because it allows you to mention veganism, not as a foreign concept, but as a compliment to their identity. This chapter is dedicated to finding that common ground and using it as a platform to break through their natural resistance. I'll use *friend* as a generic term to encompass anyone you are trying to help go vegan or to take that first step towards a life of compassion and non-violence.

Feel free to use multiple different categories as well. You may have a friend that is a huge foodie and who also runs marathons on the weekend. In this case, you should pull strategies from both the foodie and athlete categories as tools you can use to get the discussion going. Further, if you don't think your friend falls into any category, many of the strategies can still be used. Just because they don't fall into the foodie category doesn't mean they don't enjoy a nice restaurant once in a while. Use techniques from any and all categories as you see fit.

THE ATHLETE

"You have to get 1g of protein for every Kg of mass." "Plants are an inferior form of protein." If you know an athlete, you can almost bet you have heard some version of those two statements. For years I don't think you could even mention gaining muscle without saying *lean protein* in the same sentence, which implied eating chicken, eggs, and fish. Luckily, times have changed and not only are there more vegan athletes than ever, but many of them are also fairly famous. More importantly, that's great for you because you have living evidence that the old "skinny vegan" label is long outdated.

My favorite go-to reference is American Olympic weightlifter Kendrick Farris. Kendrick is a monster whose diet breaks all the rules for weightlifters. Not only does he follow a plant-based diet, but that golden rule of 1g/Kg is out the window too. Kendrick says instead, "You could say to yourself, 'Well, I get X amount of protein.' But the real question is how you feel when you consume that because training and recovery have to be at the top of the list."[1] Kendrick isn't the only athlete that would tell you the high protein requirement is a myth; my friend and author Robert Cheeke, mentioned earlier, would tell you the same.

Thanks to the work of Dr. Campbell in *The China Study*, we know that the human body doesn't need an overwhelming amount of protein to survive or thrive.[2] Around 10 percent of calories should be protein and that is significantly less than the 1g/Kg that is the typical standard—or worse, many times that amount is misspoken as 1g/lbs. High levels of protein are not only toxic to the body but contribute to health complications like kidney stones and osteoporosis, as your urinal system attempts to discard all that extra protein.[3] The conclusion is that you don't need that much protein to be an incredible athlete. You just need to consume enough calories to meet your training requirements. So now that you have an answer to the most pressing question you are going to get asked by your athlete friend, here are some ideas to get them to ditch the animal protein for good.

First, be the role model. Be healthy and be fit! If you are knocking it out at the gym or crushing six-minute miles, then no doubt your friend will take notice. What if you're not really into that? No worries, then just like I mentioned above, drop some of those famous athletes into your conversations. Is your friend a runner? Ask if they have ever heard of ultra-marathoner Matt Frazier. I had the good fortune to meet Matt recently, and he is a machine. For a perfect birthday or holiday gift, get that person a copy of his book *No Meat Athlete*. It could be the one thing that makes them decide to give the whole vegan thing a chance.

Something else you can do is to challenge them. Every athlete, including myself, loves to be tested. Ask them if they will try plant-based for a week or two, or do the 22-day challenge at Challenge22.com. Ask them to try it out just to see if there is a difference in their performance or recovery time. Another great tactic is to make a case not only for human athletes but for animal ones as well. A ton of companies try to advertise their products using animals as mascots to show strength or speed, but more often than not those animals are vegan too. The strongest mammals on earth, like elephants and bulls, are all vegan, which should say something about the perception that eating meat somehow gives you the attributes of meat-eating carnivores. The reality is that you don't get anything other than a ton of cholesterol and chronic illness by eating other animals.

When it comes to your athlete friends, I think you'll find them much more open to new information and interested to hear about the benefits of a vegan lifestyle. Most are health conscious and eager to learn more about nutrition. They will be especially interested that many of the standard practices out there are more myth than fact. So challenge them and ask how they know how much protein they are supposed to consume. Ask if they got that info off some bodybuilding website or a peer-reviewed medical journal. Help them to think outside what they know about a plant-based diet. Many of your friends may quickly realize that they have been a victim of advertising rather than performance-based nutrition.

THE ANIMAL LOVER

We literally all know someone that loves animals. There is no measurement of households with pets, but you can pretty well guesstimate that at least half of homes have at least one pet. We all love our pets, and many people will be quick to tell you how much they love animals. So when someone says to you, "I'm an animal lover," it should be a requirement for you to ask right back, "If you love animals, why do you eat them?" Sure, it's a very direct comment, but there are few opportunities to connect the dots like consistently responding to comments about loving animals than with this question. Why? It forces that other person to verbally acknowledge each time they make a choice about which animals they care about and which they allow to be killed. In short, it's a powerful way to start breaking down that wall which has been set in place by years of advertising and cultural conditioning.

My main point is that if you know someone that has a lot of pets or even has one pet they think the world of, you have the opportunity to use that as the key to opening the door of the reality that is the meat and dairy industry. Their high level of empathy for their own pets should be triggered once exposed to any kind of media that shows the suffering and torture farm animals are forced to endure. Now the big question you should have is, "How do I get that person to view those kinds of videos so that they can see what happens?" Should you stand outside their house with an iPad playing *Earthlings*? Probably not the best way, right? Really, it's as easy as saying, "I know how much you care for your own animals; have you ever thought about the animals who end up in the slaughterhouse?" If they say no, ask if you can describe the process to them to spark their interest. If they answer "Yes," then ask how they feel about the suffering of the animals, and is their pain justified if we as humans have no requirement to eat animal products? Will they be hesitant about this conversation? Absolutely. They may shut you down entirely or just walk away. However, you will be making progress by getting them to think about the choices they are making and how that impacts other beings.

How about one more way of helping your animal lover friend to think outside the comfort zone. Do they support any causes like "Save the Whales" or "Help the Polar Bears?" Much like making an appeal to their pet's freedoms and enjoyment of life, the same appeal can be made for all animals. If your friend is an advocate of protecting sea turtles by eliminating plastic straws or cutting up plastic soda rings, is it not reasonable to ask why they exert so much effort to help one animal while choosing to kill and eat another? In the same way, if you are having a conversation and the topic of, "Isn't it horrible that such and such animal is going extinct (or was killed)?" don't be afraid to throw out that question of, "Why do you feel bad about this animal and not a farm animal?" It's a tough question because there can really only be one answer, which is that they personally value one life while not valuing another, otherwise known as speciesism.

One final note. By reading this, I have no doubt these directly confrontational responses seem harsh, and, well, they kind of are. Thus, it really is upon you, the reader, to add the emotional buffering into the conversation. That is to say, don't respond to them condescendingly or with charges of them being a hypocrite, but instead be genuine and curious as to why they have never made the connection or refuse to do so.

THE ENVIRONMENTALIST

Documentaries like *Cowspiracy* and *Before the Flood* have opened the eyes of many and helped to show that being vegan isn't just about health or diet, but it links into the larger picture that is climate change and environmental protection. Ask just about anyone, and I think you will find that most people want to protect the environment. A massive campaign in the 1980s really helped to bring about a new generation of thinking by pushing the phase I mentioned earlier—"Reduce, Reuse, Recycle"—into schools, and even lesser efforts, like the TV cartoon *Captain Planet*, had a major impact on young kids like me growing up. So it's not surprising to discover that in your efforts to help others go vegan, you have an opportunity anytime you see someone recycle a can or drive to work in his or her new hybrid car.

How you can get the conversation going is as easy as making them feel good about the choices they have made, and then allowing the discussion to naturally run into the inevitable intersection that is the meat industry. For instance, if you praise your friend for driving a hybrid car, you almost certainly have to talk about the fuel that it saves and the reduced pollution that results. It would be at that point you can interject and say, "It's wonderful that you are making a change that will help to reduce the second-leading cause of greenhouse gas." If you say that it's the second-leading cause of greenhouse gas, there is almost certainly no person on Earth that can resist asking, "Well, what's the number one cause then?" You and I know that animal agriculture is number one, and now you have a logical opening to make your case and provide them the resources to further investigate. Also, now that you have established their credibility as a pro-environmentalist, they will undoubtedly want to keep up that reputation, and you have given them the means to do so.

There is another type of environmentalist you might encounter, which is the "If cows just ate grass" environmentalist. When confronted with the *grass-fed beef* environmentalist, the premises of their response is going to be that the world will be fine if cows can eat their natural food instead of flatulence-causing corn. A simple search on the USDA website says that a cow needs about 2 acres of grassland for yearlong feeding—1.8 to be exact.[4] With approximately 1.5 billion cows in the world right now, that would equate to 2.7 billion acres of grassland for each cow. The latest United States Geological Survey (USGS) estimates there to be 4.62 billion acres of farmland worldwide currently being used. I don't have to do the math for you to see that using 2.7 billion acres of the available 4.62 billion total just for cows doesn't leave much left for anything else.[5] This is also not to mention that without that fatting soy and corn diet farmers feed cattle to "finish them," you end up with leaner cows, and hence, need more grass to produce the same amount of beef.

Okay, so that's a lot of math, and you're probably not going to remember all of that, especially not on the spot when confronted with the grass-fed challenge. So here's the strategy: as I always say, don't try to win the war during one conversation, but inquire how much land it would require if everyone were to consume grass-fed beef. It's enough to get the other person thinking and hopefully doing a little research of their own. Then the last comment should be the thing that makes the most sense: "Rather than trying to drastically increase the amount of grazing land available, would it not make more sense to stop continually breeding and providing for billions of animals we have no physiological need to consume?" The answer, of course, is yes.

THE DIETER

How many people do you know on diets? A hundred? A thousand? Basically, everyone you know, right? In today's society, calories and junk food are abundant, and in kind, so are most people waistlines. Rare exceptions to the mainstream are vegans. In a 2006 study of BMI among different diets (vegan, lacto-ovo vegetarians, pesco-vegetarians, semi-vegetarians, and non-vegetarians) researchers found that vegans had the lowest, a whopping five units less than the non-vegetarians.[6] In short, that old adage about "skinny vegans" can now be used to your advantage.

One of my favorite things to hear is when friends or coworkers are talking about cutting carbs to lose weight. Pretty fit myself, I never miss a beat to say, "You know, all I eat is carbs." The looks and responses I get are hilarious, at least to me, but still, the point makes contact with the other person that, "Hey, if you want to lose weight, being vegan might be a good way to do it." Now, I know you're thinking that veggie carbs are way different from the processed carbohydrates in white bread, cakes, etc., and you are absolutely right. If you want to drop the fat, you still have to cut the calories, and most people understand that to be true. However, that doesn't refute the reality that vegan foods, in general, have significantly fewer calories, and calories from fat, than their meat-based counterparts.

So here's the main focus: if you have a friend, family member, whoever, that is trying to drop the pounds, don't miss an opportunity to suggest they cut back on foods high in fat and calories, namely meat and dairy products. Instead, recommend foods high in nutrition and lower in calories like beans, tofu, tempeh, grains, potatoes, squashes, and more. If you also happen to be at a low body weight, you have a leg up because you can, in so many words, make your case using yourself saying, "If you want this body, just eat like me." If you aren't exactly in the low BMI category, no reason to hold back either. Why not say instead, "Hey, I'd like to drop a couple of pounds myself; maybe we can both do it on a whole-foods, plant-based diet." You could even make it a competition to see who loses the most with your friends.

One last note about something I like to point out to anybody on a diet that I see consuming milk products—i.e., skim milk, Greek yogurt, cottage cheese, etc. The sole purpose of milk is to grow a 100-pound calf into a 1200-pound cow. If there was one thing you would not want to consume on a diet, one would think that dairy would be at the top of this list, since it is loaded with fat, sugar, and lots of growth hormone. It's a small comment that might open other doors, or at the very least get your friend to consider why he or she is consuming something designed to bulk up a baby cow.

THE FOODIE/CHEF

I, like many, am a foodie. I love to travel around and make it a point to try as many new restaurants and different types of food as possible. One of my favorite things about going vegan, and maybe yours as well, was going to the store for the first time and picking out all kinds of new plant-based foods to try, even though there was quite a bit less to choose from back in 2012. On social media and in our local vegan groups, few things get as much excitement as a new vegan cheese coming out or a new company with a product made just for vegans. This excitement doesn't have to only be limited to you and your vegan friends, though; no doubt you have lots of other people in your life who love to try new foods and restaurants. Have you branched out to have them try your weird vegan foods? Do you hype them up and sell them off as something special that only vegans can have? I do this all the time.

This is not an advertisement for these companies, but I love the products, so I have to mention them—not to mention that they make for good stories. A year or so ago I found vegan jerky online. The Louisville Vegan Jerky Co. and their Caroline BBQ was so good that I had to bring it into work. You can imagine the eye rolls I got from my coworkers when I brought out this package of vegan jerky, but they all tried it. You never would have expected, and neither did I, that everyone absolutely loved it. They loved it so much that my friend, who also happens to be a foodie, went on to their site and ordered the largest variety pack they had so we could try them all. Although I haven't got him to ditch the meat yet, he still loves that jerky, and every bag he eats is one less life that had to be taken.

Just the same, Tofurkey is a big hit with many people, and I like it quite a bit myself. I happened to bring in a package one day and shared some around. "Wow, this is really good!" My other coworker was almost ecstatic about this seemingly common vegan staple. To my surprise, she liked it so much she actually went on a hunt for it from store to store—there just happened to be a small shortage in the area at the time—to get more, finally finding a package at somewhere around the fourth or fifth store. Moral of the story is that you never know what might be that one thing that turns others on to vegan foods, so if you can, share with your friends.

That brings me to my last tip, which is to talk it up and make it sound like more than just some soy pressed into a patty shape. If they ask what's in it, and it's not allergy related—of course, don't try to kill someone—say "Don't worry about it, just try it!" Instead of saying, "You need to try this coconut milk ice cream," use the company name and say, "Have you ever had SoDelicious? It's freaking amazing." If you have a chef in the family or a friend, ask if they can make you something with your favorite Gardein product or exotic jackfruit. As someone who loves to cook, who could resist making something with a new ingredient? You get the idea. Add some prestige to your favorite foods to get others to try them, and hopefully, they will want to try more. Also, if any of you work at these companies, feel free to send me stuff for free advertising… just kidding! (Okay, not kidding)

THE FEMINIST

Feminism has been around for decades, and today, in its third wave, feminism is focused on significant issues like the movement against sexual assault, the worldwide liberation of women restricted by religious and cultural laws, and the continued pursuit of equality in pay and opportunity. As so many feminists strive for equality for all women, many vegan feminists have taken up the fight for females of all species. The intersection of animal rights and feminism is evident because the overwhelming majority of exploited animals are female, including all dairy cows, sows, and, the largest group, hens.

They are female for access to their breast milk, they are female for their ability to breed, and they are female for their perceived docile nature. Thus, there is a clear opening for any discussion with your feminist friend to ask the question, "Do you think women's rights should apply to female animals as well?" Obvious topics that can be brought up are sexual assault and reproductive rights. Again, I recommend you not use the term *rape* because of the strong association with human trauma. It's not the same experience, especially regarding the emotional pain inflicted during human assaults. However, that doesn't mean that what female animals are subjected too is any less valid either. They, too, experience aspects of pain and suffering with the root cause being the same, which is that their bodies are being exploited for someone else's benefit. The animals are forcibly penetrated while restrained, the process is often violent and causes injury, and the victims are left confused and frightened. Unlike human victims, every animal is made to endure a full pregnancy, only to have her offspring taken away. This process is repeated for their entire lives until they are no longer physically capable. Ask your friend what they think about these fellow female beings being forced to endure five, six or more pregnancies; is this acceptable?

Female animals who are sexually assaulted may have a slightly different experience than humans, but many of the aspects remain. Without a doubt, the most exploited are cows and sows. Cows are forcibly bred over and over to sustain milk production in devices called rape racks, a narrow, chute-like device in which cows are restrained. In an attempt to improve their family-friendly appeal, dairy farms now refer to the devices as breeding boxes, although they are the same thing. At the end of the pregnancy, the calf is taken so as not to consume any of the valuable milk and fed formula instead. If the calf is female, she will likely be raised as a future dairy cow. If the calf is a male, he will be placed in a veal crate, unable to move, and butchered within days or months. A select few calves may be raised and killed for beef when they are only a year and a half old. When a cow can no longer handle the repeated pregnancies, they often drop to the ground in exhaustion. The term "downer" was coined to refer to a cow that can no longer stand on its own strength, often a result of recurring pregnancies. Their reward for enduring so much pain and suffering is to be violently dragged or mechanically lifted away from the farm and killed.

For pigs, the experience is even worse. Sows are often placed into gestation crates, where they are unable to move for months on end. In these creates, they suffer health problems such as ulcers and pressure sores from lack of movement, and will likely spend over half their lives, most while pregnant, confined in them. Can your friend imagine themselves, or others, imprisoned and unable to move during their pregnancy? After giving birth, the piglets are removed after only a few weeks, fattened, and killed.

While the majority of the victims are female, male victims also face issues related to feminism such as unrealistic masculinity stereotyping. Domestic bulls, for instance, are often gentle and non-aggressive; however, many bull species are selectively bred to make them aggressive for sporting events like rodeos and bullfighting. This not only endangers those who have to handle these animals, but attempts to promote the idea that males are naturally violent, that it is socially desirable, and that the most aggressive males are to be praised.

All that said, the primary strategy is just to make sure animals are included in the feminist discussion with your friend. Other topics you can bring up include the strong link of dairy products to breast and ovarian cancer, how the occupation of livestock farming is dominated by men, or about how advertising seeks to strip away any female qualities and instead showcases them as promoters of the products they ultimately give their lives for—The Laughing Cow cheese comes to mind. You should strive to help make the connection that our fellow female beings are just as vulnerable to abuse and gender-based violence as us, and they too deserve a voice to speak for them.

THE PERSON OF COLOR

If you look around on social media, and even in your local vegan groups, you might notice a large proportion of white members. The disparity is so noticeable that memes and comments abound that being vegan is only for rich white people. Therefore, I think it necessary that special attention and commitment should be made to reaching out to all persons of color. If you are a person of color, then you already have insight into the differences that can arise, and I hope you still find this section useful, but more an acknowledgment that we all need to work harder to be more inclusive. If you are not, I hope you make a concerted effort to reach out to everyone, not just those who seem to fit the typical white-vegan stereotype. We all rise faster together.

Why persons of color often find it difficult to make the transition is a large and complex topic, and there are several other books and blogs that address the issue. However, looking only at strategies to get the conversation going, we can go over some of the broad factors at play. From my perspective, there are two barriers that often prevent persons of color from making the jump from omnivore to plant-based: cultural pressure and economic status. This is clearly not to say that all persons of color are impoverished or that they have a drastic culture difference from non-persons of color. What I am saying is that they may have additional or different barriers from what your life experience has been, and if you want to have a lasting impact, you may have to engage someone differently than you might have thought.

For instance, many African-American families have a culture of consuming "soul foods," many of which are heavily animal-based. So to confront someone who is African-American and say, "You need to quit eating chicken fried steak and have some tofu," can be the equivalent of saying, "You should give up your culture and adopt this foreign culture instead." So don't suggest your friend give up a part of their culture, but instead help them to embrace the best it has to offer. Instead of telling them to try some tofu, which is usually associated with Asian culture, suggest things like vegan mac n' cheese, gumbo made with beans and okra, or biscuits and vegan sausage gravy, which your African-American friend is already familiar with. Unless, of course, they love Asian food. Then by all means suggest some tofu or order some for them to try! You can also suggest things that they may not have had but are a part of their culture. One of my absolute favorites that is also vegan and a huge part of African culture is injera, a staple Ethiopian pancake of teff flour, with mesir wot or Azifa, which are lentil dishes that are commonly eaten with injera.

In other words, don't just suggest foods that you like and complement your identity, but consider your friend's cultural identity as well. If you have a friend that is of Indian descent, suggest they opt for the tremendous amount of vegan Indian dishes that are available. In the same fashion, if you have friends that are Asian, Latino, or just about any other heritage, they undoubtedly have foods in their culture that are 100 percent vegan. This will help to show that being vegan is a part of their cultural identity too, and it's more likely that their family and friends will be more supportive of the changes they are making.

In the U.S., the poverty level among persons of color is drastically higher than that of white Americans, and the same is true in other countries as well. The 2017 poverty rate for African-Americans in the U.S. was 22 percent, and for Hispanics, it's nearly the same at 19.4 percent, compared to 8.8 percent for non-Hispanics whites.[7] If you are privileged and can afford to buy vegan sausages at $8.99 a pack, and you suggest them to your friend but they don't have the financial means to afford them, they are going to think that being vegan is out of their means. Vegan fake meats and cheeses are costly—we can agree on that—but they are also heavily processed and usually fall in the category of junk food. While sometimes they aid the transition from animal products to plant-based whole foods, they are also overall unnecessary.

Consideration should be given to providing resources like recipes and animal product alternatives that are high in nutrition and don't break the bank. There are tons of recipes, like soups and stews, which use whole foods, such as lentils or beans, as main ingredients, that are not only nutritious but also affordable. So if you know your friend is unlikely to afford a bunch of specialty vegan foods, help them out and provide recipes that utilize healthy staples. The same goes for non-food products as well, like cheap plant-based alternatives to fashion or home products from recycled materials.

One last strategy is to focus on health. Just like we all have cultural differences, we also all have health risks that tend to run in certain ethnicities. For instance, in the U.S., African-Americans have a 33 percent higher death rate from heart disease than white-Americans, and Hispanics are 50 percent more likely to die from diabetes than white non-Hispanics.[8,9] You can let your friend know much of the reason for the higher rates of death and disease has nothing to do with race but instead has much more to do with diet. Higher consumption of animal products by persons of color worldwide has had a significant adverse impact on mortality. Even in Asian populations that have typically had lower death rates, the adoption of a Western diet is causing higher rates of chronic disease and death. A diet high in animal products is a trait no ethnicity should want as part of their culture, and even if it has been in the past, it no longer needs to be in the future with so many culturally-acceptable options available.

So now you have some ideas on how to get your friend interested while still allowing them to keep their personal identity. One more thing: while getting your friend to go vegan might be your number one concern, don't forget that they have a lot of race-related issues going on as well. If your initial pitch is that they should go vegan for the animals, you could quickly find yourself in a discussion about how race issues are much more important to them instead. While it's true that animal rights issues are also human rights issues, it can be hard to make that connection while social, economic barriers prohibit people of color from getting good paying jobs, or while they suffer from higher rates of incarceration. In other words, it's difficult to care about others' lives, while struggling to make one for yourself. So you might consider leading with health topics or encouraging your friend to try plant-based foods that are accessible and convenient.

THE RELIGIOUS

A large population of the world is religious, and unless the person you are trying to convince is non-religious or Buddhist, there is a good chance you will run up against an argument that their God has commanded that it is okay to kill and consume animals. In Christianity, this comes from the Bible where God decrees that every moving thing is food. In Islam, animals get more protections from the Qur'an, specifically from exploitation or mutilation; however, the eating of halal animals is still allowed and widely practiced. For both, the natural tendency is to fight fire with fire, especially if you are of the same religion. For Christianity, a typical reply is that the Garden of Eden was vegan and that we were originally all designed to only eat plants. Which is quickly countered with other scripture, and so it goes back and forth. I cannot even begin to describe the number of times I have seen this played out on Facebook and the end result is always, "Well, that's your interpretation."

As someone that is very familiar with a variety of religions and their scriptures, as well as debating religious viewpoints, my advice to you is to not engage in a battle of scripture wars. The reason is really quite simple, which is that much of the scripture used today is vague, contradictory, and worse, unfamiliar to those trying to employ it. So it becomes a never-ending spiral where each person attempts to find random verses to support their own viewpoints or logic, usually veering far away from the original discussion. The result is most discussions end up in an *agree to disagree* conclusion, or worse, with both persons upset and put off by the whole conversation. So how about a better strategy?

Many would argue that one of the central tenets of all religions is to teach or provide moral guidance, and I would tend to agree with this as well. Similarly, another fundamental teaching is to treat others how you would want to be treated, and most importantly, not to kill others. These cornerstones of religion give you the opportunity to provide a solid rationale, no matter the belief, that since we don't need to kill animals to survive, proven by the fact that you and I are still alive, that killing them for sheer pleasure is immoral. By holding to this position, you no longer need to be an expert in scripture or have a doctorate in religious study since you hold a moral high-ground.

The basic discussion, when it is appropriate, would come down to a simple exchange where you would ask "Is it moral to kill an innocent human being?" Notice the key word *innocent,* so there is no discussion of capital punishment, etc. They should answer "no" to this question. If they answer "yes" you might want to reconsider your choice in friends. Really, though, they should say "no," and that allows you to ask, "If we as humans have no reason to consume animals, and that in doing so actually hurts our health and the environment, is it morally justifiable to kill innocent beings?" That's going to be a hard question for them to answer, simply because a rational and impartial person would say "no" as well.

If they try to use scripture to rationalize or defend their position, hold fast to your core position that it is immoral and continue to drive the discussion back to the main focus. If your friend says, "The Bible says... ", or, "The Quran says... " simply say, "I'm not saying what is written is right or wrong, but if your beliefs are focused on the existence of a loving and moral God, then would that God see the unnecessary killing of innocent beings, human or not, as moral?" No just or moral God would create a being, capable of emotions ranging from ecstatic joy to immense pain and suffering, with its sole purpose to be mutilated, tortured, and killed. If you hold to the position of morality, then you will be able to have a productive discussion that doesn't challenge a person's beliefs, but instead aims to complement them. In this way, you are not challenging your friend's beliefs, but seeking to reaffirm the best in them, and the best is a loving God, not a sadistic one that promotes killing.

THE HUNTER

The hunter friend is going to be a whole different type of person than we have talked about before because you have to challenge their entire identity. Where I live in Florida, there are tons of hunters; you can see their pickup trucks parked along the forest line for miles. For them, it's part sport and part environmentalism. It's a validation of their ability to live off the land, a tribute to hunter-gatherers of the past, and a statement that mankind is still at the top of the food chain. The concept may be very foreign to you or make you mad, but this is the reality that will be quickly imparted to you by any hunter, along with probably the most worn-out joke ever, that vegan is an ancient term for bad hunter. Needless to say, you will likely not convert someone from hunter to vegan after talking to them for a couple of minutes.

As mentioned, hunting is more than a pastime; for many, it's an identity, so how do you even start to convince someone to completely abandon their identity? The best way might be not to directly engage with your friend in a battle of wits, but instead, promote activities that help to pull them back from the identity first, so they are more open to having the conversation. Those looking to experience the thrill of the hunt or excitement of outdoor marksmanship could engage in a host of other activities that do not involve beings who are merely trying to survive. Paintball, skeet, shooting ranges, rock-climbing, hiking, archery, and video simulators all offer similar excitement and use many of the same skills. If you like the same activities, try to get them interested by inviting them to go with you, so they break away from being solely focused and involved with hunting. You can also suggest events they can attend through social media or from flyers around town.

Many that hunt enjoy being out with their friends and often take their hunting dogs with them. It's an immersive experience that doesn't require hunting at all, so make a better suggestion. For these friends, a good recommendation might be to go with their friends to the dog park or even go on a nature walk with them. It might also be worth reminding your friend about the risks to their dog's health by participating in hunting, like their companion being accidentally shot or mauled by a frightened animal. Additionally, the presence of parasites like ticks and fleas that live in the woods can cause serious health issues that put their companion at risk.

If you're making some headway, you might ask your friend why he or she hunts in the first place, so you can get an idea of what is driving the behavior. Maybe they say that they enjoy the heritage of hunting or living off the land. A good response is to make a case for moving from the past to a more ethical future. Yes, humans have hunted for thousands of years, and we have done so with a variety of tools, from smooth rocks to AR-15s. This by no means is a reason to continue to do so, nor does gunning down a helpless animal with night vision cameras and a laser scope have anything to do with our ancient ancestors. Furthermore, you can make the distinction that our ancestors hunted for survival, while today's hunters simply hunt for sport.

As for developing skills for living off the land, let's be serious for a bit. If there was a major disaster that disrupted the food supply, you can guarantee wild animals would be impacted as well. If there is a significant drought, the animals will be affected first. If a natural disaster hits, they will face the brunt of the crisis, while humans take shelter. A better choice? If you are serious about survival, you stock up on long-lasting commodities like rice, grains, dried fruit, etc., not animal products that quickly spoil and go rancid.

"I do it because there is an overpopulation of animals," is another typical response. This is another topic that is sure to arise as you discuss with your hunter friend, as they will tell you that animal populations like deer and hogs are quickly multiplying and only hunters can save the day. It should come as no surprise that there hasn't been an overpopulation problem for millions of years until recently. The leading causes driving overpopulation of these animals have been the systematic killing of the predators that kept a symbiotic balance and the rapid shrinking of their habitat, forcing them into human areas like backyards and farmland.

Other species have overpopulation issues, too, namely dogs and cats, yet society has seen fit to pass laws to restrict the legalized killing of them. This is an obvious counterpoint to bring up. "Why are the cat and dog overpopulations treated differently than wild animal overpopulation?" For one species, we control the population with sterilization, but for others, we allow mass killing by any means possible. So you can see the hole in their argument. There are much better and humane ways to deal with overpopulation rather than to resort to savage and violent means. Specifically, wild hogs are favorite for hunters to bring up who live in the U.S., Australia, and New Zealand because they can be dangerous if provoked and also have the potential to damage personal property.

My favorite point to make regarding hogs is that it was farming them that led to their proliferation in the first place, as many domestic pigs made the escape from Spanish and British colonial farms in hopes of a better future in the wild—hard to blame them. While violence is the obvious solution to many, it is the same solution that continues the problem. Alluded to earlier, just in the U.S., thirty million predatory animals are killed every year to protect domestic animals, which includes the domestic pig.[10] Of course there is going to be a hog issue because their predators are being killed to protect the domestic pigs. The logical answer would be to allow nature to regulate itself, but instead, humans are stepping in to kill both the predatory animals and the hogs; how does that make sense? It doesn't. In the same way, if all the wild hogs are killed, the variety of mammals, snails, birds, insects, etc. they eat will also begin to overpopulate. Then hunters will say, "We need to kill these animals too." Shooting your way down the food chain is not conservation, nor is it something to be proud of. What does work is allowing the ecosystem to regulate itself in concert with non-violent methods like sterilization.

That was a lot to cover, and I would expect their response to include at least those items. So to recap, how do you actually get a hunter to drop that rugged, outdoorsy identity and embrace their inner hippie? The first is to encourage some better activities instead that will get them to pull away from the hunter lifestyle a bit so that when you try to talk to them about being compassionate, they are not merely fighting to protect their identity. Second is to break down that "glory of the hunt" symbolism and get them to see the reality that is them going out to someone's farm, or a limited woodland region, to kill an animal that is basically trapped geologically by human development. There is no glory in killing an animal that has nowhere to go. Last, encourage them to support the variety of other methods for controlling the population that work, either by sterilization or by natural means, so they can see their efforts really are just for selfish interests rather than a societal good.

THE FASHION ICON

If you have a fashion-loving friend, you're in luck because there are lots of great fashionable vegan products. The fashion industry is no longer the fur and leather-loving machine it used to be in past decades. Already in this millennium, many of the major companies have ditched animal products in favor of hip, vegan-friendly materials. These include Stella McCartney, Vaute Couture, Cri De Couer, Matt & Nat, Olsenhaus, John Bartlett, Umasan, Melie Bianco, Dalia MacPhee and Miakoda, Jill Milan, and so many others. Needless to say, it should be easy to suggest to your friend to ditch that leather Louis Vuitton purse or Coach wallet and get an eco-friendly alternative.

Maybe the best way to do this is to get some new threads or kicks yourself and show them off. I got a cork wallet over a year ago and every time I pull it out people stare at it and ask, "What is that, cork?" I normally say something like, "Yeah, pretty cool, right? The best part is that it floats too." It's a great segue into why I ditched my leather wallet.

While my wallet is sustainable, my dress work shoes are not, as they are made of some kind of oil-based material. It has rarely happened, but you might get that person that says, "I don't see how that's any better to use oil instead of animal products." On some level they have a good point. I think most of us are not fans of chemical-based products, which have little hope of composting. A lot of times, however, like with my dress shoes, there isn't an alternative available, so given the choice of oil-based or cruelty, I chose the lesser of the evils, in my opinion. To those kind of people, I express my hope that better options will be available soon.

Although my dress shoes are a specific item with few alternatives at the moment, there are thousands of other products that are not oil based. My Saucony running shoes are cloth and, honestly, are some of the best shoes I've ever owned. The best part is that they cost less than most running shoes do because they are made of cloth, so you even save money. Not only that, an easy way to get your friend hooked on cruelty-free fashion is to buy them a gift so they can experience how wonderful the products are for themselves.

THE MACHO

Having spent much of my life in, and working for, the military, I have met endless men and women that portray this stereotypical macho image. Is your friend the macho type? An easy way to tell is if they: 1. Wear a baseball cap all the time. 2. Wear Oakley sunglasses on said baseball cap. 3. Drive a large truck or SUV with zero purpose or need to have one. Okay, is that a requirement? No. It sure seems to be a common theme, though, and I often wonder if I didn't miss some kind of memo along the way, or a hat and sunglasses starter kit.

Really, though, the macho type is probably going to the be the typical meat and potatoes eater that loves bacon, could never give it up, and wants you to know all about it. They know that real men, or women, eat a lot of meat, have lots of leather products, and are at the top of the food chain. Know who I'm talking about yet? I'm sure you do because we all know someone like that.

So how do you try to work your way into an honest discussion instead of just getting a kickback from the macho façade? You probably won't have to wait long to find yourself in a debate, since no doubt they will make some comment like, "I could never give up meat," or, "Your food is what my food eats." All these kinds of statements open the door to ask some easy, although loaded, questions. For instance, if your guy friend says, "Real men eat meat," then you can ask, "Why would a tough guy like you eat something filled with estrogen?" After all, you and I know that meat and dairy are loaded with estrogen, and in fact, 60 to 80 percent of estrogens in the typical Western diet comes from those two sources and contributes to obesity.[11]

To that "I have to have bacon" comment, you might ask, "Do you know where bacon comes from?" If you didn't know, it comes from a pig's stomach, but you might not know that their belly and a human belly are not quite the same. If you have a female pet, you might take a look at theirs, and you are sure to find many sets of nipples running down their underside. That beloved bacon is actually just pig breast tissue. It would seem to me that there would be nothing macho about consuming pig breast tissue, which is also filled with large amounts of estrogen.

Besides the high estrogen content, animal products are also high in saturated fat and cholesterol. As mentioned earlier, continuous consumption of these two substances leads to clogged arteries, which not only affects the commonly thought of heart, but for men, the often forgotten penile artery. Surely, there is nothing macho about having erectile dysfunction, a point you might bring up if your male friend thinks bacon is the key to happiness.

These are just a couple of replies to some comments you might get, but to make a lasting impact, you will have to help change your friend's perception of what is "macho." To do that, you want to create a new ideal of macho for them. Instead of someone that uses others, namely animals, for personal gain, make it known that what's macho is protecting others from exploitation. Have you ever seen a fireman save a kitten from a tree on TV? That's macho. Is confinement and torture of a helpless animal, just so you can eat something filled with cholesterol and saturated fat, macho? Of course not.

In the same way, start building up a new image of what is macho for your friend by praising actions that are genuinely heroic, such as donating time at a sanctuary, protecting animals from abuse, and choosing environmental options that help to build a future for younger generations rather than contribute to pollution and global warming. If you have a macho or athletic vegan friend, invite them over so your non-vegan friend can see that not all vegans fit a particular image and that there are others like them that made the jump. If you don't have any, you might reference the athlete section for ideas.

There are more things you can do that will help your friend make the jump from macho animal products to macho plant-based products. There are tons of vegan jerkies on the market, and not only do they make a great gift, but they help to keep that tough image without the cruelty. Macho vegan skincare products are available everywhere that smell and work great, while ditching the unnecessary animal-based ingredients. There are even vegan leathers, made from things like mushrooms, which keep that vintage look.

THE DIAGNOSED

This might be the most relatable category on which to build a case for going vegan since we as humans all seem to have medical issues, and often they stem from poor dietary choices. The goal here isn't to play doctor but to provide resources that the other person may use to discover if their medical issue might be related to poor eating habits or improved by adopting a plant-based diet. Without a doubt, two of the most prominent medical conditions are heart disease and diabetes. If your friend or a family member has either of these two diseases, there is literally a wealth of knowledge that you can pass to them about the benefits they would get from going plant-based, and possibly even reversing them altogether.

The only diet ever proven to reverse heart disease is a plant-based diet, as mentioned earlier.[12] You can suggest to the other person that they do some research into Dr. Esselstyn on his website, Dresselstyn.com. That's a free plug because I have literally met so many people that were on the brink of dying and were able to back the disease off thanks to Dr. Esselstyn. Subsequently, they not only adopted a plant-based lifestyle but after becoming more aware of the ethical issues involved they became vegan for the animals as well. The key is just getting the other person interested in a plant-based diet, and a good steppingstone for that is to tie into diet recommendations from organizations created to combat the disease. The American Heart Association, for instance, has a "Health Living" section on their website heart.org that is filled with recommendations to eat more fruit and vegetables.[13] While it does has some animal products listed, the focus is clearly to eat more plants, and that works in your advantage to make a case for going vegan.

The same can be said for diabetes. If you go to Diabetes.org and look under Food & Fitness, you'll find the big pitch here is to eat "diabetes superfoods," which consist of "non-starchy vegetables, fruits, legumes, nuts, seeds, and whole grains."[14] If you have a friend that has diabetes, how easy is it then to make a pitch for reducing or ditching animal products altogether? The same can be said for numerous medical conditions such as autoimmune diseases, cancers, skin conditions, gastric issues, and so forth. An important thing to keep in mind is not to sell going vegan as a cure, although it could potentially have that effect, but as an additional tool that can be used to help reduce symptoms.

The best way to do this, as mentioned in the "Your Parents" section, is to take the time to listen and get a good idea of what the other person's medical condition is, and then make a recommendation of a resource that could benefit their condition. You can say something like, "I've been looking up ways to reduce my own heart disease risk and found some great information. Since you care about heart disease too; would you like me to share some of it with you?" Right there you are describing why it is important to them, and you are also making the case that you both care about health. Now you have the opportunity to share all kinds of great resources that promote going vegan, since so many of them tout a plant-based diet as essential to good health and disease prevention.

THE VEGETARIAN

Last but not least, this may be the easiest person to convince because, like Bon Jovi sang, "We're halfway there!"[15] Really, though, if you know someone that is vegetarian or you can get someone to try going vegetarian first, taking the last step to being vegan is so easy. Maybe in the past going from vegetarian to vegan was asking a lot, which was undoubtedly due to people's love of cheese. Now, however, there are tons of vegan ice creams, vegan cheeses that are amazing, and even whipped cream in a can—the options are endless.

So don't be afraid to ask your vegetarian friend what is holding them back from going vegan. It's likely they are already aware of the ethics about eating meat, so if they don't know how horrible the egg and dairy industries are, you can share a wealth of info that would help them to see the full picture. If it's just based on food preference, take them to the store or buy them some alternatives to try. With so much now available, it would be hard for them to make a strong case against going vegan, other than for convenience—which is hard stance to defend given the cruelty of the egg and dairy industries and having given up meat already.

CHAPTER 5
ANSWERS TO TWENTY COMMON OBJECTIONS

THIS CHAPTER IS dedicated to giving you the knowledge you need to answer many of the hardest objections people have when questioning a vegan diet. It's impossible to address every single objection someone could have in this book, so instead, I have provided the most common and difficult ones that I see online and have been asked while doing outreach. The big thing to remember for answering objections is to first take a deep breath and be compassionate, understanding, and really listen to what they have to say. When faced with new ideas, it is common for others to challenge them and try to reaffirm their current beliefs. Remember, the other person is not your adversary, and this should not be a heated debate, but an opportunity to hopefully share some ideas that grow long after the discussion has ended.

It is a chance for you to share your knowledge in an inclusive manner and to make a positive impact. You can help visualize the discussion by mentally putting yourself in the other person's shoes. How would you want someone to answer your questions? Would you want them to attack you with responses like, "Well, dummy, you should know that's not true because this, that, and this other thing," or would you rather they respond with "I'm glad you asked; I had that same question." Don't be the preachy, self-righteous vegan stereotype; instead, be a compassionate mentor and friend and speak from a heart of kindness.

1. WE NEED ANIMAL PROTEIN TO SURVIVE!

Their objection: "I have to eat animal foods because protein is essential for humans."

Clearly, humans do not need animal protein to survive. Otherwise, there would be no vegans, as we would have all died years ago. Whole grains, vegetables, and beans provide more than enough protein to stay healthy. Most people actually overeat protein, which stresses your kidneys as they excrete the excess in your urine or gets stored as fat. Cases of protein deficiency that don't involve starvation are nonexistent. The idea that humans need to eat large amounts of animal products is very much a Western concept, as globally 76 percent of the population derives most of their daily protein from plants.[1] The idea of "needed animal protein" is not based in science, but instead a long-standing advertising campaign that was put in place to help sell meat products. A great question to ask when this topic arises is, "How much protein do you think you need?" Statistics are on your side that the other person will have no clue. An NPD survey found that 71 percent of consumers have no idea how much protein they should consume.[2]

As mentioned before, the ideal amount is 40-50g of protein—or around 10 percent of calories—for an average person, and any additional protein will only be expelled from the body or added as fat, the complete opposite of what most people are trying to accomplish.[2] A simple formula is .8g of protein per Kg of body weight for non-athletes or a non-pregnant/breastfeeding adult. Every plant contains protein and foods like beans, grains, and nuts are all-stars in the protein department. Several plant-based foods are complete proteins, meaning they have all nine amino acids that our bodies can't produce. This includes such foods as quinoa, buckwheat, soy, seitan, chia, and hempseed.

Now the big difference between plant protein and animal protein is what comes with it. With animal protein, you get all sorts of saturated fat, cholesterol, added hormones, and antibiotics. Now compare that to plant protein which is packaged with antioxidants, fiber, minerals, vitamins, and phytochemicals.

Your response: "Every animal on Earth, from elephants to lions, gets their protein originally from plants. Not only does every plant on Earth have protein, but when you're eating plants you don't ingest the large amounts of cholesterol, saturated fat, and trans fat you get from consuming animal products."

2. ISN'T SOY BAD FOR YOU?

Their objection: "Soy is filled with estrogen, makes you feminine, and stunts your growth."

Soy is a superfood and one of the many vegan foods that are also a complete protein. A myth that has been circulated for years is that soy feminizes boys or stunts your growth, both of which are false. Soy does contain estrogens but they are beneficial isoflavones (phytoestrogens), not mammalian estrogen. Only animal products contain mammalian estrogen—in particular, milk from pregnant cows. Although soybeans are amongst the most abundant sources of phytoestrogens, they are found in many other foods as well, such as apples, rice, carrots, mint, ginseng, beer, oats, sesame seeds, flaxseed, lentils, and pomegranates.

From the National Cancer Institute: "Phytoestrogens in the human body are relatively weak and can actually bring benefits, such as a lowered risk of cancer, by 'blocking' actual estrogen."[3] These phytoestrogens actually bind to estrogen receptors, taking away spots for your body's estrogen to bind. This is important because high levels of estrogen in the body are suspected to increase the risk of developing breast and prostate cancer.[4] So it's clear that soy does precisely the opposite when it comes to estrogen, by actually reducing the amount in the body.

As for growth, your genetics and environment, and especially the presence of malnutrition, are almost solely responsible for the determination of your height. The primary sources of the soy-growth myth stem from two places: the association of soy products with Asian populations, who are the primary world consumers of soy, and a 2017 study that found an association between consumption of non-dairy milks and shorter height. In 2013 a study looked at why child height in India lagged behind that of child height in Sub-Saharan Africa and the conclusion was that environment, namely food allocation to children, was the main factor.[5] The same has been found for that of Asian children, who have often faced malnutrition because of limited resources and large populations.

The 2017 study done by principal investigator Jonathon Maguire, MD, has been found to be profoundly flawed—not to mention that Maguire also has strong connections to the dairy industry. Maguire's research has received financial support from the Danone Institute and the Dairy Farmer's of Canada, and he has authored other studies funded by the Dairy Farmer's of Canada that promote dairy consumption.[6] A central point from the study was that non-dairy milks do not provide enough protein to fuel growth and pointed to the low amounts of protein in almond milk. While almond milk does have limited protein content, it's ridiculous to clump all non-dairy milks in the same boat and point to the lowest denominator of the bunch. Soy milk has 8g per 8 oz. vs. the 1g per 8 oz. in almond milk; that's even more than 2 percent dairy milk, which only has 7g. Clearly, the study should have named soy milk the winner! The main takeaway is that children who are consuming adequate calories are almost always meeting nutritional requirements needed to meet growth needs, as seen in the India vs. Africa study.

Your response: "Only animal products contain mammalian estrogen, not plants. Your height is determined by your genetics and your environment to include nutrition, and is not related to a simple food choice that is part of a much larger diet profile. "

3. SOY GIVES YOU BREAST CANCER.

Their objection: "My Mom had breast cancer, and I was told to avoid soy because it can cause breast cancer."

If you have a friend who is at risk or is a survivor of breast cancer, they are likely to hit you up with this common objection. The soy-breast cancer connection is based primarily on soy being associated with estrogen, as discussed above, and on a 1998 study in mice that showed soy isoflavones could cause breast tumors to grow.[7] So we already know that estrogen and phytoestrogen are not the same and that phytoestrogens can actually protect you from some cancers, one of those being breast cancer. More recent studies, not based on mice, have confirmed that soy is not linked to breast cancer and actually acts as a protective and preventative agent, boosting longevity in breast cancer survivors. One particular study showed that women who ate the most soy have a whopping 24 percent lower risk of developing breast cancer.[7] An additional study found that "Women from both the U.S. and China who consumed 10 mg/day or more of soy had a 25 [percent] lower risk of breast cancer recurrence."[7] As for your thyroid, soy has no effect on the thyroid per a 2006 study.[9]

The short answer on soy and breast cancer is that soy actually helps to protect against breast cancer, not to mention the massive amount of nutrition it packs as well; it's a true superfood. After dispelling the myths on soy and breast cancer, you have a great opportunity to make a case to go vegan to decrease the risk of getting breast cancer. All the leading breast cancer prevention organizations (Susan G. Komen, Breastcancer.org, the American Cancer Society, etc.) confirm that soy provides positive benefits that protect against breast cancer and you can easily pull up any of their websites, which have sections discussing soy.

Your response: "All the leading breast cancer organizations promote that soy protects against breast cancer."

4. PLANTS HAVE FEELINGS TOO!

Their objection: "Plants are alive, too, so vegans are a bunch of hypocrites because they're killing living beings."

If your eyes aren't rolled way back in your head, then you are doing better than me the first time I heard this comment. It may seem like a joke, but you would be surprised to hear that there are people that see no difference between plants and animals. Clearly, plants are structurally very different than we are as sentient beings. They do not have a central nervous system or a brain, which means they cannot feel pain in the sense we are accustomed to. Yes, they are reactive to stimuli and responsive to their environment, often evident as they grow towards sunlight, but they are not conscious in any way. Additionally, the fruit they produce is quite literally grown for the sole purpose of being eaten so that the plant's seeds can be dispersed. Personally, I would not spend too much time engaged in this discussion, since most of the time the topic is brought up for reaction rather than to have a real conversation.

Your response: "Plants lack a brain or central nervous system, so they do not experience pain as we know it; they simply respond to external stimuli."

5. IT'S TOO EXPENSIVE.

Their objection: "Fruits and vegetables cost too much. Only rich people can afford to be vegan."

As previously mentioned, you absolutely can go broke buying a bunch of specialty vegan items. Field Roast make some mini corn dogs that I am especially fond of that are also quite expensive. However, the same is true of any food. Specialty meats can cost nearly $100, organic milk is as much or more than most plant-milks, and most seafood seems to cost a fortune. Eating plant-based foods, however, doesn't have to be expensive, and the options become drastically cheaper when buying non-certified organic. We could have a whole discussion of organic vs. conventional, but we could agree, I'm sure, that both are a better and healthier option than processed animal-based products. Rice, beans, potatoes, and frozen veggies are all cheap options that can fit in any budget.

One of the biggest reasons many animal products are reasonably priced at all is because many governments subsidize them; that is to say, the government pays the farmers to keep costs low with your tax money. Thus, the more we as a society move to a plant-based menu, the more these subsidies will move over to our favorite fruits and vegetables instead. I personally would love to see avocados and bell peppers for fifty cents each!

Your response: "There are plenty of low cost, highly nutritious plant foods, and you might even save money by no longer purchasing expensive animal products like seafood and luxury meats."

6. A VEGAN DIET IS UNHEALTHY.

Their objection: "I saw an article online where a child died because they were fed vegan food, so clearly being vegan is unhealthy."

Simply eating plant-based foods is not going to ensure you are eating healthy food or getting complete nutrition. If you eat nothing but vegan cookies, you will undoubtedly be in poor health just the same as if you ate non-vegan cookies. However, when it comes to overall health, eating a fully nutritional meal as an omnivore, vegetarian, or vegan are not equal. From a famous 1978 Adventist Health Study, a vegan diet could help you live up to ten years more. Ten years! If that isn't healthier, I'm not sure what else is.

How about one more study? In a study published in the JAMA Internal Medicine Journal, scientists at Massachusetts General Hospital monitored the health and diet records of more than 130,000 people for thirty years. They found that "every three percent increase in calories from plant protein was found to reduce the risk of death by 10 percent […] The figure rises to 12 percent for risk of dying from heart disease."[10] We can safely say from both studies that eating a nutritious diet is critical to being healthy and that a vegan diet has proven itself time and time again to be the healthiest.

Your response: "Any diet can be unhealthy if you fail to get complete nutrition, but studies have shown a whole-food, plant-based vegan diet to be healthier than one that involves eating animal products."

7. WHAT ABOUT ALL THE SUPPLEMENTS VEGANS HAVE TO TAKE?

Their objection: "If you have to take a bunch of supplements, then obviously being vegan isn't a good choice."

My counter immediately would be "Do you take any vitamins or supplements?" This objection is common although almost laughable since vitamins and supplements represent a $37 Billion industry and the majority of consumers are, you guessed it, not vegan.[11] While many vegans do take some supplements, it's probably not even necessary on a whole-foods, plant-based diet, because you get so much nutrition from plant foods. There are lots of apps and websites that allow you to keep track of your nutrients, and I have never seen a low amount from the foods I eat. The only exception is the infamous vitamin B12.

From the National Institute of Health: "Vitamin B12 is required for proper red blood cell formation, neurological function, and DNA synthesis." So it really is quite important, as we just read, and it is certainly true that it's an important and essential requirement for humans. What's not true is that vegans are the only ones capable of having a B12 deficiency, since lots meat-eaters do as well. An article in the American Journal of Clinical Nutrition discusses the commonality of B12 deficiency and found that "Vitamin B12 deficiency and depletion are common in wealthier countries, particularly among the elderly, and are most prevalent in poorer populations around the world."[12] The article actually goes so far as to point out that the belief that "strict vegetarians" only had B12 deficiencies was "erroneous" and it "usually takes ~20 years (sic) for stores of the vitamin to become depleted."[12] The author's end recommendation was that flour should be fortified with B12 for the benefit of everyone.

So when it comes to B12, vegans are not alone; we could all use more of it in the food we eat. Further, that's why much of our food is already fortified with all kinds of vitamins and minerals, such as iodine in salt and folic acid in bread. With so many vegan foods already fortified with

B12, there is little need for any supplements, and it is no different than how all our food is currently treated.

Another typical response: "But we need animal products for B12," or, "I'd rather get my B12 naturally from meat." B12, as you may know, is produced by bacteria in the soil, *not* by animals. What you may not know is that thanks to animal agriculture, even animals have a hard time getting B12 from the soil, since most of their food is now also processed. To remedy this, B12 is supplemented to their food as well. So the idea that meat is a natural source of B12 is erroneous and laughable. The easier and smarter way is to not involve animals whatsoever and just supplement our own diets with bacteria-produced B12.

Your response: "Actually many of the foods we eat are fortified with a wide range of vitamins and minerals, including vitamin B12 which is lacking in many people's and farm animal's diets, not just vegan's."

8. FARM ANIMALS WILL OVERPOPULATE THE EARTH!

Their objection: "We have to eat farm animals because if we don't, they will keep breeding and take over the world."

This is actually a pretty standard and sane response if you've never been exposed to a farm or read much about how they operate. Artificial insemination isn't frequently broadcast as the main attraction for several reasons, but the outcome is that most people don't even really know about it. They have no idea that on a farm the vast majority of animals are not wandering around looking for that special mate to have offspring with, but are instead inseminated in a rapid and often painful process. This makes sense, especially at a dairy farm where all they have are cows. Not only would it cost a lot to maintain additional bulls that produce no milk, but the processes itself becomes time-consuming, and there is no guarantee that all of the females would become pregnant. Thus, farmers would lose profits from having cows that failed to produce both milk and calves. To maximize profits, approximately 95 percent of dairy cows in the U.S. are inseminated artificially.[13] Similarly, over 80 percent of pigs are also bred using artificial insemination to eliminate the need to maintain a boar.[13]

Turkeys, on the other hand, are a rare case of a new and growing issue of the side-effects of selective breeding. In an attempt to grow turkeys with larger breasts, turkeys today have literally become too big to actually mate with each other naturally. This being the case, 100 percent of commercial turkeys are now artificially inseminated.[13] The end story here is that going vegan is not going to result in farm animals breeding at a record pace and overpopulating. Ironically, farmers, and by default, meat-eaters, are actually the direct cause of the current overpopulation problem that has allowed farm animals to become the dominated land-vertebrates on Earth.

Your response: "The majority of farm animals are artificially inseminated, so by reducing or eliminating meat consumption, their populations would be drastically reduced."

9. VEGANS ARE SKINNY AND WEAK.

Their objection: "Every vegan I have ever seen is skinny and malnourished, and I don't want to end up like that."

While vegans generally have a lower BMI than those eating the Standard American Diet, which is definitely not a bad thing, vegans as a whole are much more nourished than the typical person.[14] Eating a varied whole-foods, plant-based diet high in fruits and veggies, it is next to impossible to have any shortage of vitamins and minerals, and you would maintain any weight as long as your calorie intake was sufficient enough to meet your body's minimum maintenance requirements. How a whole-foods, plant-based diet differs is that the high level of fiber helps to fill you up faster and keep you feeling full longer, resulting in a tendency to maintain lower BMI.

The reality, though, is that vegans actually come in all shapes and sizes. Sure, there are plenty of skinny vegans, just as there are lots of skinny meat-eaters too. In contrast, there are also plenty of vegans who are anything but thin, such as weightlifters like Kendrick Farris, for instance. You don't have to look hard either to find a slew of massive vegan bodybuilders like Torre Washington, aka The Vegan Dread, Jon Venus, or the many others who have redefined what being vegan looks like. To the point, the old view of the skinny vegan is dead. As veganism continues to gain in popularity, it's hard not to find endless examples of vegans who are fit, massive, and powerful.

Your response: "There are endless examples of vegan powerlifters, endurance athletes, and bodybuilders, and they are anything but skinny and malnourished."

10. CAVEMEN ATE MEAT.

Their objection: "Man evolved to eat meat, and that's why we have such big brains because we ate lots of fat-rich calories."

Many factors have been suggested as to why the human brain has expanded over many millennia of evolution. While a diet high in fat, such as would come from animals, played an essential part as a food source in times of scarcity, it's much more likely that a calorie surplus played a more significant role. There is no doubt that our brains are indeed a standout among other mammals as they are drastically larger compared to our body mass than other beings. However, it may surprise you to know that the human brain is only 2 percent of your body's weight and yet consumes 20 percent of your body's energy needs, which is a massive amount.[15]

This significant energy requirement doesn't necessarily require a large level of dietary fat, but it does demand a substantial increase in calories. Unlike other beings, humans were able to slowly develop methods of farming and cooking which gave us access to these extra calories. This jump in calories, along with ever-increasing social complexity, are likely the reasons human brain growth has been so dramatic—not meat alone. After all, if eating meat was all that mattered, full-time carnivores like lions and wolves would be driving Mercedes, and we would be the ones hunted to near extinction. So that should put such an argument to bed. Calories, not meat, was the reason for our evolutionary success. Few advancements in history helped us to reach that calorie surplus like farming, which allowed us to live in stable communities with an abundance of food, rather than an unpredictable nomadic lifestyle.

While consumption of meat helped us along the way, farming helped to really turn the tide for humankind. As for the statement that "We evolved to eat meat," clearly this is not the case. While humans have been able to make meat edible through the advent of cooking, we struggle to properly digest the sugars and proteins, especially lactose (milk sugar) of which 65 percent of the world population is still intolerant to, and are made ill by high levels of cholesterol and bacterial contamination. Even the most evolved meat-eating humans on the planet, the Inuit, who have actual genetic mutations in response to a high meat diet for the last 20,000 years, are still riddled with high rates of heart disease, osteoporosis, parasites, and a reduced live span compared to even those eating the typical Western diet.[16]

All that said, we are not cavemen. We are highly evolved mammals that drive cars, talk on cell phones, and send people into space. We know that eating meat shortens our life spans, while a plant-based diet lengthens it. Even though our ancestors ate meat, that doesn't mean we must continue to do so with so many other better alternatives available that help to ward off disease and chronic illness. We should continue to evolve and consume foods that help to further our, and all species, advancement, and not merely do something just because our ancestors did.

Your response: Consumption of animal products may have aided in our survival in the past, but they only contribute to chronic illness today. Should we not choose to eat the most beneficial foods for our health instead of the limited foods of the past?"

11. WE ARE NATURAL OMNIVORES.

Their objection: "Humans are obviously omnivores, since we have been eating both plants and animals for thousands of years, and it's our benefit to continue to do so. Look at these canines!"

So this discussion is not unlike talking about cavemen. Physiologically we are capable of consuming animal products, yes, but only if the products are cooked to kill off the wealth of bacteria, viruses, and parasites or served raw under the strictest of conditions. This is entirely at odds with the many natural omnivores that do not have these requirements, such as bears and canines who routinely eat raw meat without risk of death or illness. Their bodies, and in particular their digestive tracks, are genuine products of evolution, designed to quickly pull nutrients out of food in a highly acidic environment and rapidly expel the waste before these pathogens have a chance to incubate.

The human digestive tract, on the other hand, is poorly equipped to break down large amounts of animal products, often resulting in constipation. It's even worse for raw products, resulting in stomach and intestinal infections. Ever heard of people getting worms from sushi? In the same manner, we also have the ability to poorly digest a variety of products like fabrics, rocks, bits of plastic—even swallowed metal coins can make the trip. However, no one advocates eating any of these objects because it's not a matter of *if we can*, it's a matter of *should we do so*. Thus, it should be a no-brainer that the best foods to consume would be the ones that benefit us the most nutritionally while providing the least risk of illness or complications.

So when we know that animal products carry a high risk of pathogens, cause intestinal distress, and are a causal factor for our deadliest chronic illnesses, it only makes sense to consume plant-based products that carry none of these risks. Last, the obvious and most important benefit is that no fellow beings are forced to live a life of misery and eventual execution for a product that we as humans do not need and do not benefit from consuming.

Hey, hold on, what about those canines? Aren't humans clearly designed to eat meat since we have a couple of pointy teeth? You might be surprised to know that many herbivores also have canines, including humans. Canine teeth are essential for many reasons, especially for gripping on to food. Who has the most massive canine teeth in the animal kingdom? The answer isn't a carnivore or even an omnivore. It's actually a herbivore, the hippopotamus.[17] Hippos use these teeth not only for gripping large plants but also for defense against other animals. Turns out the presence of canine teeth has nothing to do with meat consumption at all.

Your response: "Humans are capable of consuming a wide variety of plant and animal products, but just because we can eat something doesn't mean we have too."

12. IT'S THE FOOD CHAIN.

Their objection: "Animals eat other animals, and humans are at the top of the food chain; it's the circle of life, and we have the right to eat whatever as the top predator."

Without a doubt, animals eat other animals, but they often do so because they have no other source of food. Cheetahs, lions, wolves, and others have no choice but to eat the only foods they have available. Humans, on the other hand, have many different plant-based foods to choose from. Since we have these alternatives that are just as good or healthier, there is no reason to continue to kill animals for food.

As for being the top predator, we have achieved what no other species on Earth has even come close to doing. We have clearly established ourselves as having the ability to dominate all other animals, but that certainly does not give us the moral right to do so. By exerting dominance over all the world's real predators, such as large cats, reptiles, and canines, we have actually destroyed the so-called "circle of life." By killing these animals, we have disrupted the ecosystem and created environmental emergencies, allowing what were once prey animals to rapidly breed while remaining unchecked by their natural adversaries.

This "might makes right" way of thinking works in no other frame of reference throughout history, but somehow when applied to animals, it is deemed okay. Powerful governments, corporations, and individuals all have the ability to dominate other humans with lesser resources. The big kid at school can dominate the smaller kids in their class. In all of these scenarios, we as humans stand up and say this is wrong! We don't allow the more powerful to exploit the weaker members of our society just because they can. Should we not also do the same for all animals? As the only animals on the planet capable of such global influence, humans have an obligation to preserve and ensure the continued survival of all Earthlings, and not to simply exploit them for temporary personal gain.

Your response: "Animals kill each other out of necessity, but humans have other alternatives."

13. GOD GAVE US ANIMALS TO EAT.

Their objection: "My religious text says God put animals on the Earth to be my food; who are you to contradict God?"

Although we talked about this a bit already, it's such a common and difficult question to answer that I have included it here as well. Again, you should not make an attempt to fight scripture with scripture, since it's a losing battle that will undoubtedly end in verse fighting rather than changing someone's mind. Instead, go after the foundation upon which all religions are built: morality.

With no necessity to consume or use animals for any purpose, is it moral to kill another being capable of all the same emotions and physiological responses as us? Is it right to imprison our fellow beings and subject them to what would be called torture if they were instead human beings? Animals value their lives, form friendships, feel pain, and fear death just like humans. No God would give animals all those qualities only to let them suffer in silence simply for human pleasure, and allow all this while the consumption of these animals is simultaneously responsible for the destruction of the planet.

No matter their beliefs, the foundation of religion, and society for that matter, is a stance against violence unless it is necessary to protect yourself from harm or stay alive. We live in a world where plants are readily available, and we can end world starvation by simply making a different choice. Would God want us to continue letting millions of people starve to death while breeding and killing billions of defenseless beings, or make a simple change? The answer is clear, right? Since there is no necessity to kill or consume innocent animals, it must be immoral to kill for pleasure and convenience, especially if the cost is our fellow human beings starving to death.

Your response: "Just because a religious text says you can, doesn't mean you have to, and without a reason to kill our fellow beings, it is immoral to do so for pleasure."

14. CARBS MAKE YOU FAT.

Their objection: "Eating all those carbs will just make you fat; I have to eat lean protein for my diet."

I swear I hear this all the time, even when being vegan isn't the topic. Someone at lunch or dinner will say "No thanks" to bread or rice because "I'm trying to watch my carbs." I've always found this mind-boggling because you always hear that vegans are skinny, etc., yet the majority of the vegan diet is carbs! You would think someone would make the connection, but that never seems to happen unless I speak up, being fairly slim myself, and say, "Hey, literally all I eat are carbs… look at this body!" Which is usually followed with a cop out like, "Well, you just have a fast metabolism." It's a good comeback, though, and kind of humorous as well, and if you, too, are on the thinner side, it's worth throwing out there. However, I know that we all come in different shapes and sizes and being vegan certainly doesn't imply that we are all health nuts or gym rats. So what can you reply with? Usually, people forget that there is a big difference between junk food and whole foods, so merely pointing out that difference is enough to provide a gentle reminder that carbs are an all-inclusive term for weight gain.

Your response: "Are you talking about processed/refined carbs or whole-food complex carbs? Because whole foods like fruits and vegetables are primarily carbohydrates and are some of the most nutritious, highest fiber, and lowest calorie foods you can eat."

15. EATING OUT IS IMPOSSIBLE.

Their objection: "I could never go vegan because it's inconvenient."

As a vegan, I'm sure this is an easy ball for you to hit out of the park since it's a daily must to figure out where you are going to eat on any given day. If you're more of a junk food vegan, this might be the easiest question you get all day because you will be familiar with all the different fast food options available. The big recommendation I would give is to ask what kind of places they eat at now. If there are options available at some place they already frequent, the odds are high the next time your friend hits up that restaurant they might opt for the vegan option just to try it out; this versus asking them to go to an all vegan restaurant which could seem intimidating and outside of their comfort zone. Once they dip their toe into the vegan waters, don't abandon them! Make sure you continue to provide places that have options tailored to their tastes, not just yours, and show your excitement when they make the decision to get a plant-based option.

Your response: "There are tons of vegan options everywhere; tell me, what places do you eat at now, and I can make some suggestions for you to try the next time you go?"

16. I EAT ONLY ORGANIC, GRASS-FED, HUMANE MEAT.

Their objection: "I agree with you that factory farming is cruel to animals and bad for the environment, and that's why I only eat free-range animals that are treated well by local farmers."

Sitting in a bar in Santa Fe, NM, a new friend of mine told me this exact statement, and to be honest, I was somewhat uncertain of what to say to her. She was convinced that the animals she paid to have killed for her next meal were living a life of luxury at the farms near her house in the countryside. All the animal products she bought were free-range, hand-fed, living in a utopia of extravagance, cared for by a hard-working farmer who just absolutely loves animals. Yes, we both know that this is almost certainly a load of crap and that even if it weren't, in the end, these animals would still be killed as babies or young adults in the same manner as those in the worst factory farms, likely even being sent to the same processing facilities. So what do you say?

Luckily her recounting of how well the animals were treated took an absorbent amount of time, so I had a while to contemplate how to break down this wall of disillusion that had been built up by marketing and whatever else, without discouraging her desire to actually make a difference. That's an important note as well, that, as much as I didn't want to hear her talk about basically still killing animals, she really wanted to make an impact that would increase their quality of life, and that's a pivotal position to make use of. So how you can get them to make that mental leap from free-range to freedom is to stay focused on the basic fact that it is both immoral and unnecessary.

Is it better than factory farming? Yes! Is it better than these animals living a normal and free life? Of course not. Our pets also live comfortable and good lives, but if I loved them one day and chopped them up for food the next, even my non-vegan friends would be horrified. That's the crux of the discussion; good treatment still does not justify killing another being when there is no necessity to do so.

Your response: "If there is no necessity to kill another being, then regardless of how well they are treated, isn't it still immoral to kill them? Doesn't that just make them value their life even more?"

17. WHAT IF YOU'RE ON A DESERTED ISLAND?

Their objection: "But if you were on a deserted island with just a pig, you would eat it right?"

This probably seems like a stupid question, so why does it get asked so often? While you might be tempted to say "Yes" or "No" depending on the direness of the situation, the real motive behind it is that it's really just a trick question. If you say "No," then it allows you to be painted as a crazy vegan that would rather die than survive. If you say "Yes," then, well, you're really not that vegan after all, are you? I've been asked this question before and I, like most, fell right into it; but you don't have to. The best answer is to either say "I'm not on a deserted island," and try to move on, or to fire back with your own ridiculous question like, "I don't know, if we were on the island together, would you want me to cook and eat you?" This way you shake loose the boundaries of such an entrapping and ridiculous question, as well as add in some humor. Don't let the other person try to get you with a made-up reality; make up your own in response or invalidate the question.

Your response: "But you and I are not on a deserted island, and even if we were, the chances are high it would be filled with edible plants."

18. I CARE ABOUT PEOPLE FIRST.

Their objection: "That's great you care about animals, but kids are starving to death, and people are living in poverty; we need to take care of them first, not limit what food they can eat and what products they can use."

This response is called a red herring. A red herring is an argument fallacy where instead of discussing the topic, the other person goes off on a tangent, raising a separate issue to avoid addressing the issue at hand. In this case, part of the tangent is to also make you, as an animal rights activist, look like you could care less about your fellow humans, and that you only care about animals. Luckily it's easy to bring the discussion right back to the issue because animal rights issues are human issues. Yes, there is worldwide poverty and children do die from starvation every day; it's absolutely horrifying. In the U.S., 70 percent of the grain grown "Is fed to livestock—that's enough grain to feed 800 million people."[18] That's a fast fact from Appendix A. A majority of the plant food the world grows goes to feed livestock rather than the world's impoverished people.

Additionally, the global impact of breeding and maintaining billions of animals, as I'm sure you know, has a massive impact on the environment and contributes to the massive rise in greenhouse gases. While this affects everyone on the planet, the most vulnerable are the ones who suffer the most consequences. As temperatures increase and ocean levels rise, it is those with no resources who face displacement from climate disruption or death from drought in their fields. The end point is that these issues are directly related and it should be easy for you to bring the discussion back to animal rights because it's a human rights issue as well.

Lastly, while many human issues are important, they are often complex and can't be solved easily by an individual. Child labor, war, and genocide are all human rights issues that need to be addressed, but it will take more than an individual to do so. What the other person *can* change today is their personal habits. Instead of consuming a product that has directly resulted in the death of another being, three times a day, he or she can make the choice to stop. Additionally, this same response can be used for other red herring arguments such as "Animals are killed while harvesting grains" or "Killing bugs makes you a hypocrite." Both of these arguments seek to derail the discussion at hand. The main take-away is there will always be other issues, but the other person has the power today to change what ends up on their plate.

Your response: "There are lots of problems in the world but reducing consumption of animal products is one that you can solve today."

19. IT'S PART OF MY CULTURE/HERITAGE.

Their objection: "Every year my family has turkey for Thanksgiving dinner, and I don't want to give that up."

Consumption of animals is part of just about every culture, religion, and holiday celebration. Whether it's Christmas or Canada day, you can bet someone has a family or local tradition that involves animal products. As discussed a bit in Chapter 3 about culture for Persons of Color, an essential response is not to focus on what the other person shouldn't have, but what they can have instead. You don't want to give the impression that the other person has to give up their culture or traditions, but rather make different choices that are a part of their culture. Thanksgiving in the U.S. is always a hot topic because the holiday entirely revolves around eating a dead turkey, and for many, the family pressure to not partake in the meal is almost overwhelming.

How you can help the other person to overcome this objection is to help them find a way to make different choices in the environment they will be faced with and arm them with the knowledge to gain acceptance. For instance, the first Thanksgiving never even involved turkey, but instead included wild game, bread made from maize, and lots of vegetables like turnips, carrots, onions, garlic, and pumpkins.[19] So if they are concerned about having to tell their family, "I don't want any turkey because I'm vegan," a response sure to get a lot of negative feedback, they can say instead, "I think instead of turkey, I'd like to try eating some other traditional holiday foods." This response can drum up a bit of a different conversation, one not focused on vegan versus culture, but concentrated on expanding foods that are a part of their family's tradition. This same maneuver can be used for all kinds of holidays and celebrations.

Your response: "You don't have to give up holidays or celebrations with your family at all; what other plant-based foods are typically enjoyed during that time?"

20. BACON! I LOVE THE TASTE OF MEAT.

Their objection: "I love the way meat tastes and I could never do without it. You eat what you want and let me eat what I want. "

This is about the hardest objection you can get. After all, if someone doesn't want to make a change, you certainly can't force them to. You might think of this as the final trump card to end any more discussion, but in reality, it's probably the last defense the other person has left. They might be very close to finally accepting the overwhelming evidence that their consumption and use of animal products is destroying their health and the environment. The take away is *Don't Give Up*, because it's likely that if you're at this point, you might be on the verge of breaking down the very last barrier they have.

What you can do at this point is ask for a little bit of effort. If the other person is genuinely fed up with the discussion, a small peace offering is tempting. Ask if they would be willing to try just one vegan meal a week instead of giving up those things right away. Ask if the other person could just replace one thing, like swapping plant milk for cow milk, and focus in on that. You'd be surprised how willing most people are to give a little effort just to end the mental gymnastics of trying to defend a lifestyle they know is built on killing other beings.

Another counter to this last defense is to ask, "Does pleasure justify killing?" It's a difficult question to respond to now that the discussion has boiled down to the foundation of why most people continue to eat animal products. Knowing that it is bad for health, bad for the environment, and causes pain to other sentient beings, it's hard to justify killing them simply for pleasure. If they say "no," then there should be a positive connection going on. If they say "yes," then you can easily ask about the morality of killing other animals or people for pleasure; which should get a "no" response. Then you can ask the same question... because the only real answer is "no."

Your response: "Is it morally okay to kill another being simply for pleasure?"

WHY ARE YOU VEGAN?

This last question is not an objection but something you will inevitably be asked. For a long time, this question was the hardest for me to answer, just because there are so many reasons why I went and will always be vegan. You could jump into a long discussion about the environmental impact of consuming animal products, you could talk about how it helped your health condition to improve, or you could respond with lots of other reasons. When I am asked, "Why are you vegan," my response is simply, "Because it is unnecessary to exploit other beings." It's a straightforward reply that leaves the door open for lots of other questions.

Whatever your response is to this question, try to think about it before you get asked, so you have a clear and thought-provoking answer that encourages others to ask more.

CHAPTER 6

PERSONAL STORIES

I've told you many of my personal stories, but thousands of others have found their own ways to help others ditch the animal products and take up a compassionate lifestyle. I received lots of their stories from all around the world, and I want to share some of them here, in the hope that you will find inspiration and encouragement that anyone can make a difference. Each story is in the person's own words. They took the time to share what they thought was important for you to hear, and what strategies worked on their friends and family.

Each story shares a little background on how they became vegan and how they were convinced to make the change, or how they convinced someone in their life to make the same change. Many of the methods they used you are ones you have already learned here in this book, and now you can see them in action. I hope they show you that no matter who you are or where you live, you, too, can help those around you to make the connection and go vegan.

Reign – @ReignOverYouMusic
Toronto, Ontario – Canada

I've been vegan just over four years now, and it's forever changed me. As soon as I was introduced to the facts, I went from a self-proclaimed "cheese lover" to a morally-consistent vegan all in one day. Since then my reasoning hasn't changed but my approach has changed drastically.

When I started sharing veganism with my friends and family, I was almost ashamed of my lifestyle change. I don't know if it was from years of brainwashing or self-doubt, but I was a pushover. I let people eat animal products around me, held my tongue, and only talked about veganism when asked. Do you want to know how many people I influenced this way? One. He was my boyfriend and more plant-based than vegan. It was a strange way to live, as I was—and still am—an outspoken, passionate, honest person. Luckily, with time, this changed. I went from believing everyone was on their own "path," to believing veganism is the moral baseline. Now, when someone eats something not vegan, I tell them how I feel about it. When someone asks if they can bring an animal product in my house, I say "no." I really thought I'd lose people in my life but guess what? I didn't lose one person! Instead, people started asking questions. People were interested and wanted to learn more! I quickly learned the most important thing I've ever learned about humans. People want to do the right thing. Finally, I found the key! How many people do you think wake up one day and say "What a beautiful morning! Can't wait to be a cruel, selfish person today!"? Not very many! It's nice to live your morals.

How do you show people around you veganism is the right thing to do? Know your facts and do your research. Whether they want to help animals, the environment or care about their health, all the facts are on the side of veganism. When I get asked a question, I have an answer. If I don't have an answer I'm honest, do my research and get back to them with the facts. I encourage and love an open debate! Debating has been a fantastic tool to help open the minds of others. I am careful only to use facts I can prove and to stay away from an emotional debate. To play to the emotional side, I find *Earthlings* to be an amazing tool.

Okay, so now they care about the animals, and they know all the facts. So what's left? One of my favourite ways to help with the transition is to make veganism delicious and fun! Usually, the most important and sometimes first step is showing everyone how easy this life can and will be! I host dinner parties, bring food everywhere I go, I have a vegan food Instagram, and take my friends to the best vegan restaurants around. If veganism isn't easy and delicious, you're not doing it right! Show them it's an easy decision, because it is. Be loving and confident in your choice, and you will only succeed.[1]

Andrie D.
Montreal, Quebec – Canada

My coworker was a vegetarian. So many times I had talked to her about the horrors of dairy and eggs during friendly conversations, but she would just say, "I know it's sad but blah, blah, blah." She never seemed to want to go further even though she had been vegetarian for over ten years. This really annoyed me because she always claimed to be vegetarian for the animals.

Even after I left my job, my former coworker and I remained good friends and kept hanging out. One day we decided to go out to eat to a vegetarian (mostly vegan) restaurant, and it just so happened that restaurant was not far from an all-vegan market that I knew about. I needed to pick up a few things, so I asked her to come with me. When she walked inside her eyes lit up like a little kid's on Christmas morning. She was like, "Oh my, I never knew there were so many vegan things out there. There's cheese, whipped cream, ice cream, chocolate bars, pizza, everything! Everything I love but vegan." I was like, of course! Companies can veganise just about *anything*. So she bought a lot of things.

That night she told me, "You know, I thought veganism was restrictive; now that I know there are all these alternatives, I'm excited about trying it." I was excited for her too. I even gave her a ton of recipes so that she could make her own plant milk, cheese, etc. So it's been about five months, and she's still vegan to this day. We still talk and hang out often; I help her find vegan beauty products and house-cleaning products. Her husband that turned vegetarian with her also turned vegan; so I guess indirectly I got him to go vegan as well since he just went along with her.[2]

Maayan P.
San Diego, California – USA

I grew up in Israel and lived there till I was twenty-one. When I turned thirteen, I watched some videos of farm animals being killed and was horrified. It was so disturbing that I ditched meat and became vegetarian. I thought I was making a positive impact and still had one of my favorite foods: cheese. Not long after I happened to watch some dairy videos and realized that being vegetarian wasn't enough, I had to give up the milk and cheese as well. I decided to go vegan and went to the store to try some vegan products, one being a veggie cheese. Not only did it cost a lot but I hated it. I wanted to make it work, but in the end, I just couldn't give up the cheese.

That was until I watched *What the Health* with my sister. This time I was done with dairy and I went vegan for good. Now, years later, I again tried the newer vegan stuff that came out, and it was way better and much more available than before. What I didn't expect was that my sister, who was not even vegetarian, saw me go vegan and became interested as well. I took her to some vegan restaurants, and after trying some of the food and still impacted by the documentary, she also decided to go vegan. I was so excited for her.

My parents were harder to educate than my sister. I tried for a long time to show them that animal products were not only bad for their health, but the animals were cruelly treated and suffered greatly. My Dad, being very loving of animals, finally made the connection and both he and my Mom gave up meat after many talks about how they are treated and killed. Not long afterward they both flew from Israel and visited me at college in San Diego, CA. While they were visiting, I took them to all kinds of vegan restaurants. My Mom's main issue for not going vegan was what to cook. She is the main cook and didn't know what to do or how to cook vegan food and said, "It's just too extreme." By taking them to vegan restaurants, she was able to get ideas of what to cook and see that it wasn't as hard as she thought.

In the past, I had tried to get them to watch some slaughterhouse videos so they could see, like I did, how horrible the industry really is. Every time they refused. Instead, I got them to watch *What the Health*, and at the end of the movie, my Dad said, "I think we need to make a change." Both my parents have health issues, my Mom is 64, and my Dad is 74. I told them, "If you don't do it for yourselves, at least do it for my sisters, brother, nieces and me; we want to keep you around as long as possible." That was it, they went vegan. My Mom still struggles with the change, but I talk with her and help her shop when I go back home.[3]

Nichelle B.
Laveen, Arizona – USA

On November 6th, 2017, I decided to watch a documentary I had heard about over the weekend at a friend's party. Little did I know that *What the Health* was going to change my life forever! When I decided to make the transition, it was initially for health reasons since my father had just passed a few months earlier from a massive heart attack. He was fifty-four, obese, sedentary, and had congestive heart failure. After this challenging time, I knew one thing for sure; I wanted to live longer than fifty-four! I have three children, and I plan on sticking around for a long time to see them and their future babies grow up. After watching this documentary, I was set on getting healthy. I had been to the doctor the previous month to help with quitting smoking, dealing with anxiety, and some arthritic pain in my shoulder; I figured adopting a plant-based diet could help.

I changed the way I cooked, no longer serving anything with meat, eggs, or dairy. This was a *big* change for my husband, three kids, and my mother. Fortunately, there was no argument over the change for the most part, probably because I handle all the cooking in the house. The issue that did come up was with my husband. Not about no longer eating meat, but because he doesn't eat any vegetables. A vegan who doesn't eat vegetables? Yeah, he definitely keeps me on my toes! When we first transitioned I took the time to educate myself on the vitamins, nutrients, and all the things our bodies need to survive and thrive on this way of life. Raising three small children, this is something essential to me. Having a husband who doesn't consume a whole food group that contains the majority of what we need certainly makes things interesting, but I made it a point to cater to him and allow him to eat whatever he wanted so long as he gave up the meat. To help him avoid deficiencies he takes a vitamin, OptiVega, and I sneak Amazing Grass: Green Superfoods into his smoothies to make sure he gets what he needs. While this journey started as one to save our health, it has evolved into so much more. As I was taking that time to educate myself of the nutritional needs, I also educated myself on the effects on our planet, environment, the welfare and well-being of the animals. This was a life-changing, eye-opening, stomach-dropping, gut-wrenching, tear-shedding experience, and the only thing I would change is having the opportunity to open my mind up sooner.[4]

Joshua H. – Founder of Vegans Advice
Adelaide, South Australia – Australia

Now in my seventh year of veganism, I have spent just over six of those being a "hardcore" activist. As an activist I have "converted" or "aided" over 1,000 people with their vegan journey; potentially more but these are just the ones that have contacted me directly.

It all started with my first blog on Tumblr; this is where I developed my confidence and the ability to debate with others without losing my cool, remaining calm and staying on point. I would spend hours and hours each day scrolling through the feed or looking at the "Vegans" hashtag, as that is where non-vegans would post their ridiculous arguments against a plant-based diet and veganism. The comments would normally consist of the common "plants have feelings" argument or the desert island scenario. I would respond to each and every one of them and point them in the direction of a more educated path. My favorite posts were the long ones, where people had taken time out of their day to write a long-winded post about hating vegans or had written a lengthy response to my reply. This is where I was able to take each and every point that they made, write it down, pick it apart, and really make a case for veganism.

This slowly gained more and more attention growing the account to 6,000 followers. Which at the time was my most significant achievement within the community. Through these posts, I would routinely get messages about how I helped them go vegan and through reading my responses they made the switch. Now, my greatest accomplishment is my friend Kat. We were internet rivals, you could say, regularly commenting back and forth and she would always have something to say about my posts. A few years later (after leaving Tumblr) I received a message on Facebook from Kat saying she had finally made the switch and was now vegan.

From Tumblr, I made a move over to Facebook as I had seen the ability to grow pages quickly and reach larger audiences. I decided to create my own page and named it "Anonymous Vegan;" it was a darker page where I would share the ins and outs of the animal abuse industries whilst also sharing vegan information, help, memes and more. This page grew quickly and with it so did the responsibilities. As the page grew so did the number of messages that I would receive about people taking on a vegan lifestyle and how the page had helped them. The page grew to 35,000 likes with posts being shared thousands of times, videos having millions of views and hundreds upon hundreds of messages. I've rebranded my Facebook page, and it's now Vegans Advice. I have a new blog at VegansAdvice.com and a podcast in which I talk about veganism, animal rights and more. I still continue to help people go vegan, and opened up my pages to other activists to help them spread their message and help others.[5]

Cynthia R.
Mobile, Alabama – USA

I have two children, my son is seven, and my daughter is four. From the time my daughter was born she has always been fussy, bloated, spitting up, and a very light sleeper. She ate constantly and was always uncomfortable. Her doctor tried all kinds of acid reflux medications and never once did a test to see if it was actually that. Fast forward to when she was two, and all her problems continued and got worse. When she got her teeth in, they were brittle and so was her hair. We could not let her hair get past her ears because it would break off. She ended up in the hospital because every time she went to the bathroom for months, there was blood. We were there for three days, and they never figured out what it was. When we got home, I was on a mission to find out what could be done.

At home, she did not get better. I was trying to eliminate anything that could be causing her this pain. We tried everything, but when it came to gluten-free stuff, I kept coming across vegan stuff on Pinterest. It was the strangest thing. I had never encountered veganism, so over the next few months of trying to wrap my head around it and my daughter not getting any better I decided to give it a try. Like for real, I thought it was impossible, but I did it, and it did not kill me, I was shocked! I started my kids on it and the most beautiful thing that could ever happen happened for my child, she got better. She rarely has pain and can finally enjoy being a little kid.

My husband and grandmother, who also lives with us, were not happy about us being vegan. At first, they both made ugly jokes, and it rubbed off on my oldest for a bit. Slowly with time and a lot of cooking and talking to my husband he came around, mostly because we are parents and we cannot be on different pages. He chose to support me in the choices that I make for our family. He is also not home much, so I make most of the decisions for the family, a benefit. As for Meemaw she loves it now and got over herself a bit—persistence paid off. She says she feels better, her health is getting better and can hardly tolerate when she is not eating a plant-based diet.[6]

Nathan B.
Seattle, Washington – USA

My first exposure to the idea of not eating meat happened when I was in my early teens. I was staying in a shelter and some Seventh Day Adventists came to talk to us. They made the point that animals don't want to get slaughtered, and the stress hormones they produce impact us when we eat them. While I didn't make the connection yet, this encounter planted a seed in my mind. One of my counselors at the shelter was vegan and a member of Food not Bombs. He talked about the animal industries with me, never criticizing me but just discussing the concept. I really looked up to him, but I still didn't get it. I think if he had been a little bit more persistent I would have made the switch. I've always loved animals, and I'm not quite sure why it took so long for me to realize that I shouldn't eat them. I think for me, I didn't really want to accept the reality of what my dietary choices meant for others.

A year or so later, my neighbor sold his house, and the woman who moved in had a son about my age who I became friends with. Talking with him was what got me to stop eating animals. I don't think he had to say much. He showed me some literature and gave me a copy of *Diet for a New America*. It all made sense, and I stopped eating meat completely; although, I still ate dairy and eggs for another year.

My transition to veganism was quite sudden. We were at a protest at the Seattle Fur Exchange. I realized that if I was holding signs and yelling at people to stop killing animals for their skins, while continuing to support the dairy and egg industries, I was a total hypocrite. I went vegan the instant I realized that, and haven't had any second thoughts about it. That was roughly twenty-four years ago.[7]

Eugenie G.
Cape Town, Western Cape – West Africa

In 2010 I started dating the man who is now my husband. At the time I was already pescatarian, in part due to my father who praised and supported my choice. My husband ate meat and growing up in a conservative home had never considered the alternative. I never asked him to stop eating meat or even told him that it bothered me. I did, however, convince him to see some photos and video clips of animals in factory farms and slaughterhouses. In 2012 one evening I called him over to watch a video clip of pigs in gestation crates. I got up to make some coffee and when I returned to the room and he looked up and said, "I will never eat meat again. I will from now on be pescatarian like you." He never ate meat again.

My grandfather had been a dairy farmer in 1950s and told me that the way that he produced milk was that a calf would stay with his mother and after months when the calf was naturally weaned from the cow's milk he would continue to milk her and this way she would continue to produce milk. So I assumed that milk was always produced this way. I also always believed that when eggs were labeled free range it was ethical because these came from chickens eating grain and running around in a big, green field.

Also in 2012, I was told by a friend that I had misconceptions about dairy and eggs. I began to research it and when I learned the truth, I made a decision. At the end of December, I told my husband that on the 1st of January I will give up eggs and dairy. He asked me why, and when I explained it to him he said that he would give up eggs and dairy too, and he did.

We still ate fish occasionally. Fish had always seemed to be different from other animals to me, and I had no idea what overfishing was doing to our oceans. I watched *Cowspiracy* one day while my husband was at work. There was a scene of a fisherman gutting a fish that was still fully conscious as it struggled to get away. That scene still haunts me. When my husband got home, I told him that I am giving up fish too. He asked why and I told him to watch *Cowspiracy*. Afterward, he quietly said, "I'm not going to eat fish anymore either."

Since then I have learned what fishing does to all marine life and exactly how bad commercial livestock farming is and what it is doing to my health. I no longer see meat, fish, eggs, or dairy as food. I also try to not be judgmental when I talk to others, but I find it difficult when somebody knows the horrors and continue to support the industry.[8]

Raluca C. – Founder, Pieces of Heaven
Timisoara, Timis County – Romania

I live in Romania, and while there are not many vegans here, the numbers are growing every year. I started my charity, Pieces of Heaven, because I wanted to make a change in the world and I know I need more people to work with me to make a difference that counts. My charity helps animals and needy families in Romania. The purpose is to educate people and help others in need. We are the link between the ones in need of help and those that can help. In the future, I plan to create a sanctuary for a diversity of species so people can have access and contact with the animals they usually eat. This way they can see how beautiful and lovable they all are and veganism can be promoted in a kind, attractive way.

In Romania, we still don't have many vegan options in supermarkets and restaurants, so if you don't have the time to cook it can be a bit difficult sometimes. However, if your motivation is strong, you can stick to veganism pretty easily. I have been able to convince many people to go vegan myself. Most of them started by just cutting out meat and then the dairy also. Some of them are volunteers in my charity, others are friends and even ex-boyfriends. For all of them, I think the biggest reason they decided to become vegan was they saw how passionate I am about life and happiness of animals. They all love animals too, and I just helped them make the connection. I invite the people interested in a vegan lifestyle to my place for delicious meals and show them that it's not hard to live a vegan life. Just as important, I would tell them what to buy and from where. I even take them to meet my rescued bull.

For all my friends if they seemed interested, I would ask why they were and tell them all about being vegan. If they were still interested, I was there for them, and I told them to write to me anytime they have a question about anything. I said, "Please write to me or call me for every silly question or big question you have about veganism." They all did too, some about food, some about clothes, some about eggs from Grandma. I always tell my friends that I am very proud of their choices.

I post online a lot about veganism and talk a lot so everyone around me knows that animals deserve our empathy and all the help we can offer. The minimum we can do is not paying other people to hurt, torture, and kill them.[9]

Heather S.
New Port Richey, Florida – USA

I feel it is better to lead by example rather than try to convince someone to go vegan. Most people are not usually open to receive so much new information. For example, my husband did not go vegan until one year and eight months after I had. For 622 days I watched him consume meat and dairy. It saddened me more than anything. I wanted to force him to watch documentaries and cry out loud how horrible his actions were, but I knew that would not be effective.

Instead, I chose my words carefully to not put him down. When I spoke about anything vegan related, I did so gently. It was the sparkle in my eyes he noticed when veganism got brought up. He saw how passionate I felt about it. After all that time, he realized that I was serious. Becoming vegan was one of the most important things I had ever done. This was not a diet or a phase; this was a lifestyle change that I am committed to. It was my choices and actions every single day that showed him it could be done and he could do it too. I showed him that it is possible to unlearn and relearn everything we had been taught. It is possible to change your entire way of living because he saw me do it.[10]

Jessica G. – Owner and Founder of Jessica Rose Stitchery
Myrtle Beach, South Carolina – USA

When my boyfriend Tyler and I met, I was a vegetarian of two years, and he was an avid meat eater. I worked at Bojangles at the time (my first high school job) and would often bring him home boxes of unsold chicken, bacon, etc. to avoid it going to waste. I had talked to him about vegetarianism a few times, but he was not at all interested. He could never, and would never, stop eating meat, he said.

A few months later, his meat eating was starting to really bother me as we got more serious in our relationship and I continued trying to convince him to stop eating animals, but nothing I said got to him. He watched the videos, he listened to my reasons, but he still wanted to eat meat. He always thought he couldn't live without it because it was all he had ever known, growing up eating animals and their secretions. This was normal for him, as it is for most of us.

By this point, I was desperate to get him on board, so I challenged/dared/bet him he couldn't go one month without meat. I basically forced him into it, promising it would only be for a month, then he could go back to eating meat. He *very* reluctantly agreed, with much nagging and convincing on my part. I noticed him cheating a few times at first, sneaking some meat here and there, and thinking I wouldn't see. So I refused to kiss him after he ate it, pulling every trick I had up my sleeve in an attempt to get him to stop eating animals.

As the month went on, he started noticing how easy it was becoming. He stopped sneaking meats and began enjoying the foods we were eating together. By the end of the month, he was feeling great, healthy, accomplished, and starting to see the truth that not only do we not need to eat animals to survive, but you can actually thrive on plants alone. Time went on and the longer he went without eating animals, the better he felt and the more he began to understand vegetarianism.

We were oblivious vegetarians for a few years (he never ate meat again) until we were behind a chicken truck one day on the way to my brother's house, face to face with the victims of animal agriculture on their way to slaughter. This was such an emotional experience, I decided then and there I needed to do more for these helpless animals; I decided to go vegan. At first, it was hard, I was unsure what to eat and what replacements to buy, but it got easier with time and became second nature, just as vegetarianism had.

We both began looking deeper into the industry and genuinely learning everything we could, about eggs, dairy, meat, animals for entertainment, testing, etc. We watched every documentary we could find on the subject, and the more we learned, the more we both regretted not going vegan sooner; thinking we were helping the animals by merely not eating their flesh, all the while consuming eggs and dairy, oblivious to the truth. Like many vegetarians, we were naïve enough to believe we could consume these products without the animals dying or being hurt, which of course is not at all true.

Today, we are both *extreme* vegans, some might say, starting to become active, and constantly advocating for the animals and veganism. To this day, Tyler will randomly thank me for forcing him to go vegetarian for a month. He says he is unsure if he would have made the commitment without me pushing him into it. Although he hated me at the time, pissed off that I was "trying to control him" or "force my opinions on him," he is genuinely grateful for me showing him the right path and leading him towards a happy vegan lifestyle free of animal cruelty.

We have both gotten several friends, family members, and a few strangers on board with veganism throughout our journey and will not stop until every cage is empty and animal liberation has been achieved. Sometimes people require a little bit of a harsh push to be able to see the truth, and they will thank you in the long run for steering them in the right direction and helping them find a better way of life.[11]

Elena I.
Lisbon, Lisbon District – Portugal

My husband Matt and I moved to Vancouver, BC after having worked in Dubai for ten and eight years respectively. A lavish lifestyle where I, as an Event Manager in one of the most prominent hotels, was pampering groups and wedding couples by selling them "swimming with the dolphins" as a highlight. I was in Germany visiting my family and Matt was in France spending time with his, while we were waiting for the Canadian Visa to come through. A German cookbook author was all over the news and social media introducing plant-based cuisine as the next best thing. I always thought that being vegan was a bit hardcore but thought it was only fair to try a thirty-day vegan challenge myself and educate myself before taking a side. I wanted to see if these vegans had a point.

The positive changes within the first week were hard to deny, and the more I read and watched about animal products and the animal's suffering, the less it made sense. We left for Vancouver, and I asked him to try out the same thirty-day challenge and see how his body responds, hoping he could lower his cholesterol and stop taking his medication at some point. When Matt was initially tested for his cholesterol, which supposedly runs in the family, it was so high that his doctor said he would not celebrate his fortieth birthday.

It was honestly more of a visual challenge for him, thinking something was missing on his plate. Within the thirty days, we watched a few documentaries together, but he also educated himself without me pushing him. Maybe, it was because we were away from family and friends, your daily influences that he felt more open to trying something new. You are somehow on more neutral territory when you are not being judged. We were "alone" in a new country, educating ourselves on a subject we never questioned. Even for Matt, growing up on a farm, he never asked himself the questions if it's morally okay what we do to animals when we don't have to. He was merely taught that it's okay.

We never had a discussion about whether or not we wanted to continue to support this industry, or if I ever wanted to promote animals in captivity again. Now, I can see that it's all entertainment, let it be to eat, to wear, to hunt, or to watch animals in a zoo, aquarium, etc. The oppression is the same, and there is always a victim, a non-willing participant.

I found veganism because I was curious, for Matt it was more of a health situation. At the end of the day, it brought us back to our innate compassion. Needless to say, Matt is now off any medications, his cholesterol is back to normal, and he is healthier than ever. We are blessed with empathy; we can put ourselves in someone else's shoes and make a decision based on that. Looking back, we are simply taught to be selective with who we stand up for.[12]

Karen R.
Los Gatos, California – USA

I've always loved animals. It's probably genetically encoded in me... my mother loved animals as well, and the few pictures of her as a child show her clutching a dog, a duck, a cat.

As a child, I would find half-dead birds in the gutter and bring them home to nurse them to health. One day, while coming home from school, I found a wounded pigeon. My father wanted to kill it, believing that I would contract a disease from the poor thing. I vividly remember screaming, crying, and begging for the pigeon's life. We—the pigeon and I—tipped the scales of mercy in his heart; he let me keep the bird, it recovered, and we both went on to live our lives.

When I was about nine years old, I became aware of the plight of harp seals being clubbed in Canada, and whales being killed by Norwegians. The sudden realization of the cruelty inflicted by the human race upon innocent animals made an indelible mark upon me. I drew a picture of seals and whales and made the rounds of neighborhood houses, collecting signature to send to the King of Norway. He never replied, but that didn't deter me. An artist, I drew endless pictures of horses and read every book about horses and dogs. I also subscribed to *Rodale's Organic Gardening and Farming* and sent money to the only animal welfare group I knew of: North Shore Animal League.

About this time, my older brother began raising rabbits in our yard to sell for meat to the local grocery store. I vividly remember hearing their screams as they struggled for their lives while he snapped their necks. This memory will never leave me.

By the age of thirteen, I had become vegetarian and cooked most of my own meals. In high school, I joined Future Farmers of America (FFA). As a vegetarian, I knew that eating animals was wrong, but it didn't occur to me to examine the system of animal husbandry and reject it. I joined because I wanted to be close to animals, and that's just the way it was done. I raised two lambs and two steers, all sent to slaughter after showing them at the county fair. I named them, cared for them, and sent them to their deaths.

At the age of twenty-five and after twelve years as a vegetarian, the man I was dating (now my husband) convinced me that I needed meat in my diet. I do believe that if more information had been available to me at the time, I wouldn't have started eating meat again.

It was fate and a close friend who played a pivotal part in my evolution into a vegan. Fast forward twenty-five years: at the age of fifty I began experiencing severe arthritis in my joints. The pain would jump around: severe throbbing, pain, and swelling, first in a few fingers, then elbow, then shoulder and so on. My orthopedist suggested all types of pills to help alleviate the pain. In early 2012 I went to him with severe aching in my hip. I asked, "What could it be?" He said, "It's normal degeneration." I remember thinking, *Normal degeneration? That doesn't make sense, I'm too young!*

A year earlier, a close friend of mine, Lynette had become vegan. A friend of hers, B.J. in North Carolina, had already switched to a vegan diet. Lynette read *The China Study* by T. Collin Campbell and transformed her whole life. She became an excellent vegan cook. Her husband and one daughter switched to a plant-based diet. During the year before my switch to veganism, Lynette was bubbling with enthusiasm about her newfound diet and principles. Every time our group of friends got together, she shared what she had learned, how great she felt, and her outrageously delicious food! Talking about a plant-based diet and animal rights was, for me, like standing in the rain after a ten-year drought. It was a rediscovery of everything I had believed years before; it had been buried under the weight of society's dictum of how people think about and use animals.

Around May 2012 I recall discussing with Lynette my terrible joint pain. She quietly suggested, "Why don't you just try not eating meat?" I did, and a week later I told her, "Hey—I'm feeling better! I still some pains though." She said, "Why don't you stop eating dairy?" I did. She explained to me, as kindly and gently as possible, the horrors of the egg industry which grinds up millions of male chicks every year and entombs chickens in giant barns where they live short, miserable lives filled with unspeakable cruelty. Three days after completely eliminating animal flesh and products from my diet, I woke up feeling strong and pain-free. It was a miraculous change from the grinding pain that had become my daily existence. That was almost seven years ago, and I haven't looked back. Once I changed my diet, my eyes were opened to the tremendous suffering of animals caught in our modern agribusiness complex.

Not everyone appreciated Lynette's newfound enthusiasm. One woman in the group became violently opposed to hearing anything about plant-based diets and even started avoiding our group get-togethers. This fierce opposition to hearing anything about veganism baffled me, but I think I understand it now. Promoting veganism is a direct attack upon people's staunchly-held beliefs and a nation that subsidizes and encourages meat and dairy as necessary to the human diet. It is literally an indictment of those who continue to support the mass confinement, abuse, and murder of innocent animals.

I'd like to say that I became vegan for the animals, but that wouldn't be the truth. I became vegan because, in no uncertain terms, my body was telling me that the traditional American diet, which included meat, dairy, and eggs, wasn't nourishing me; it was harming me, and my body was sending out alarms that only an idiot could ignore! But with the help of a close friend I made the change, and a whole new world opened up to me. My arthritic pains disappeared; I felt lighter and more joyful; and I discovered a calling that has become a central part of my life: educating others about the benefits of a plant-based diet and its closely-related principle of animal welfare and liberation.[13]

CONCLUSION

So are you ready to take on the world and make everyone you know go vegan? It's probably still pretty daunting, isn't it? The important thing is that you now have a much better idea of how to approach people, and just as importantly, how not to. You don't have to be that angry vegan protester that we all see on TV and social media. By just being yourself, really listening, being kind, and responding to the other person's objections, you are already on the path to effecting real change. Yes, your friends and family are tough, but you now know how to work around many of their defenses, so that you can encourage positive change rather than end up in a battle of wills. The best part, the more you actively engage with others, the more comfortable you will be responding to any objection in a positive and compelling manner, which invites the other person to want to learn more. You can make your friends and family go vegan, and you don't have to be perfect, you just have to try.

Whether you think you can convince your best friend or a total stranger in the meat aisle of the supermarket, every time you engage with someone, you have the potential to lay the seeds that could grow into a whole new world for them. I've met people that decided after only a couple minutes to try going vegan, and I have friends that, after years of discussion, are still hesitant to go all in. However, even those that are not vegan have made changes, reducing their consumption of animal products and making simple swaps like trading dairy for plant-milk. You can make a huge difference even if you don't get them to go all the way. That difference, the small changes, can have huge impacts on the profits of the meat and dairy industry and the policies governments make, so don't forget that every little win is a big win for the animals.

So here we are at the end. Again, thank you for convincing yourself to go vegan; that in itself is already making a huge difference in the lives of animals and helping to slow the rapid climate change our planet is enduring. Thank you for purchasing this book; just by doing so you are already helping to make others go vegan, since much of the proceeds will be used to support animal rights activism all around the world. Lastly, and most importantly, thank you for wanting to make a difference! I wish you all the best in your endeavors to help end the suffering our fellow beings have had to endure for so long. Any help I can give to mentor or support your efforts I will, so please reach out either on social media or online at *AndrewJPratt.com.*

APPENDIX A
ONE HUNDRED FAST FACTS

These are just some of the reasons you can give others why they should *go vegan*!

1. If the world went vegan today, we could feed ten billion people.[1]
2. Six billion male chicks are suffocated or ground up alive each year.[2]
3. Ten billion land animals are killed for food every year in the U.S.[2]
4. The USDA kills thirty million wildlife animals to "protect" animal agriculture.[2]
5. The USDA spends $100 million a year to kill approximately five million wild animals a year to protect commercial animals.[3]
6. We feed and slaughter sixty billion farmed animals every year; there are 7.3 billion humans on earth.[2]
7. Pasture-raised cows produce four times more greenhouse gases than cows raised in confinement.[2]
8. A plant-based diet is the only diet proven to reverse heart disease.[4]
9. Seventy percent of the grain grown in the U.S. alone is fed to livestock—that's enough grain to feed 800 million people.[5]
10. Vegans save up to 724,925 gallons of water per person each year.[5]
11. Only animal products contain cholesterol.[5]
12. Seventy percent of food poisoning cases are caused by contaminated animal flesh.[6]
13. Fifty-one percent of human-caused greenhouse gas emissions come from the meat industry.[7]

14. Ninety-five percent of our dioxin exposure comes from of meat, fish, and dairy products.[6]
15. Vegans have less acne.[5]
16. Vegans have less anxiety, depression, anger, hostility, and fatigue.[5]
17. Vegan women have a 34 percent lower rate of female-specific cancers like breast, cervical, and ovarian cancer.[8]
18. Cows can live twenty-five years, but females are killed at seven years old and males at five months.[9]
19. Chickens normally live fifteen years but are killed as forty-two-day-old babies.[10]
20. Chickens bred for meat grow sixty-five times faster than normal.[11]
21. Twenty-five gallons of water are needed to produce one pound of wheat. Around 2,500 gallons of water are needed to produce one pound of meat.[12]
22. A vegan diet activates genes that prevented disease and deactivates genes that caused various cancers and other illnesses.[12]
23. Plants yield ten times more protein per acre than meat.[12]
24. Meat eaters are 2.5 times more likely to develop gallstones than vegans.[12]
25. Going vegan could add fourteen years to your life.[13]
26. Vegans have a 78 percent lower risk of diabetes.[14]
27. Ninety-seven percent of Americans are fiber deficient; animal products contain zero fiber.[15]
28. A plant-based diet can easily provide sixty to eighty grams of fiber per day.[15]
29. Eighty percent of all the corn in the United States is consumed by livestock.[16]
30. Cheese is made with rennet (the stomach of slaughtered newly-born calves).[17]
31. Seventy-five percent of the world's population is lactose intolerant.[18]
32. Fish and Shellfish contain high levels of lead, cadmium, arsenic, and mercury.[19]
33. All commercial farm animals are artificially inseminated.[20]
34. Millions of chickens scream and kick as they are scalded alive from faulty farm practices.[11]

35. Three-quarters of the world's fisheries are exploited or depleted by commercial fishing.[21]

36. For every one pound of fish caught, up to five pounds of unintended marine species are caught and discarded. [21]

37. Up to 650,000 whales, dolphins, and seals are killed every year by fishing vessels.[21]

38. Animal agriculture is responsible for up to 91 percent of Amazon destruction.[22]

39. Humans and the animals that we raise as food make up 98 percent of the land biomass.[21]

40. Eighty percent of antibiotics sold in the U.S. are for livestock.[21]

41. Chickens form friendships and social hierarchies.[23]

42. Vegans have a 57 percent reduced risk of death from heart disease.[23]

43. Meat eaters are 30 to 40 percent more likely to develop colon cancer.[23]

44. Processed or cured meat eaters suffer from a 70 percent increase in pancreatic cancer rates.[23]

45. Meat-based diets can cause cancers of the stomach and esophagus, as well as lymphoma.[23]

46. More than half of chicken is tainted with fecal matter.[23]

47. Ninety-seven percent of chicken breasts harbor bacteria that could make you sick.[23]

48. Pigs have the cognitive skills of three-year-old human children.[23]

49. Men who eat meat are 3.6 times more likely to contract fatal prostate cancer.[24]

50. Removing red meat and dairy reduces body odor.[24]

51. Dairy product consumption increases acne.[24]

52. Kale contains more calcium than milk.[24]

53. Vegans are less likely to be stressed, anxious, or depressed.[24]

54. Sixty percent of global biodiversity loss is due to land cleared for meat-based diets.[25]

55. Turkeys live ten years in the wild but are killed instead at nine weeks old.[25]

56. Up to 90 percent of sea life caught by shrimp trawling is thrown overboard dead.[25]

57. Eighty percent of pigs have pneumonia before being slaughtered.[25]
58. Makeup brushes are made of squirrel, mink, sable, horse, or goat hair.[25]
59. Seventy percent of human diseases are linked to animal agriculture.[25]
60. All protein is initially made by plants.[25]
61. Ninety-nine percent of farm animals in the U.S. are raised in factory farms.[25]
62. Vegans have an average 8 percent lower BMI than meat-eaters.[26]
63. Total cancer rates are 19 percent lower in Vegans. [27]
64. Processed meat is a Class 1 carcinogen.[27]
65. Red meat is a Class 2 carcinogen. [27]
66. One serving of processed meat a day increases diabetes risk by 51 percent.[28]
67. Dairy is the number one source of saturated fat.[28]
68. Ninety-three percent of dioxin exposure comes from eating animal products.[28]
69. Commercial animals are largely fed GMO corn and soy.[28]
70. Dairy foods have been linked to the development of autoimmune diseases.[28]
71. All dairy food contain pus.[28]
72. Milk does not build strong bones.[28]
73. Eighty percent of all antibiotics made in the U.S. are fed to animal agriculture.[29]
74. Dairy causes antibodies in the blood that attack the pancreas.[28]
75. Approximately 90 percent of pork, beef, and chicken is contaminated with fecal bacteria.[28]
76. The largest and strongest terrestrial animals are herbivores.[28]
77. You can reverse heart disease with a plant-based diet.[28]
78. Estrogen in dairy can affect sexual maturation of pre-pubertal children.[30]
79. Two servings of red meat a day increase bowel cancer risk by 35 percent.[31]
80. Vegans have an average cholesterol level 30 percent lower than meat-eaters.[32]

81. Fifty-five percent of the water consumed in the U.S. is from animal agriculture.[33]
82. Livestock covers 45 percent of the earth's total land.[34]
83. Animal agriculture is the leading cause of species extinction, ocean dead zones, water pollution, and habitat destruction.[35]
84. Livestock operations on land have created more than 500 nitrogen flooded dead zones around the world in our oceans.[36]
85. Up to 2.7 trillion animals are pulled from the ocean each year.[37]
86. Fifty percent of worldwide grain production is fed to livestock.[38]
87. A mere 1.5 acres can produce 37,000 of plant-based food or 375 lbs. of beef. [39]
88. Vegans produce 50 percent less CO_2.[40]
89. Meat-based diets can lead to erectile dysfunction.[41]
90. Plant-based diets are associated with higher IQs.[42]
91. A vegan diet reduces rheumatoid arthritis pain and stiffness.[43]
92. Vegans sleep better.[43]
93. Vegans have more youthful skin.[44]
94. Veal calves are put in heavy chains to keep them from moving and live in darkness.[45]
95. Eighty-two percent of U.S. dairies "dock" their cow's tails.[45]
96. Ninety percent of egg-laying hens in the U.S. live in 0.6 sq. ft. of space, less than a sheet of paper.[45]
97. Chickens' beaks are cut or burned off without painkillers.[46]
98. Seventy percent of sows are kept in gestation crates for most of their lives.[46]
99. Ninety-five percent of Americans said it is important how farm animals are cared for.[10]
100. Animals want to live; they love life and fear death. [1]

INSPIRATIONAL QUOTES
ON VEGANISM

*"The worst offenders on this planet: pedophiles, sex offenders, murderers do not get treated anywhere near as badly as the way we treat the most innocent and vulnerable beings on this planet." -**James Aspey**[9]*

*"Although I have been prevented by outward circumstances from observing a strictly vegetarian diet, I have long been an adherent to the cause in principle. Besides agreeing with the aims of vegetarianism for aesthetic and moral reasons, it is my view that a vegetarian manner of living by its purely physical effect on the human temperament would most beneficially influence the lot of mankind." -**Albert Einstein**[5]*

*"On the general principles the raising of cattle as a means of providing food is objectionable, because, in the sense interpreted above, it must undoubtedly tend to the addition of mass of a 'smaller velocity.' It is certainly preferable to raise vegetables, and I think, therefore, that vegetarianism is a commendable departure from the established barbarous habit. That we can subsist on plant food and perform our work even to advantage is not a theory, but a well-demonstrated fact." -**Nikola Tesla**[6]*

"Animals are my friends... and I don't eat my friends."
-George Bernard Shaw[2]

"Eating flesh is unprovoked murder." **-Benjamin Franklin**[7]

"A man can live and be healthy without killing animals for food; therefore, if he eats meat, he participates in taking animal life merely for the sake of his appetite. And to act so is immoral." **-Leo Tolstoy**[4]

"There is no fundamental difference between man and animals in their ability to feel pleasure and pain, happiness, and misery."
-Charles Darwin[2]

"It takes nothing away from a human to be kind to an animal."
-Joaquin Phoenix[1]

"I personally chose to go vegan because I educated myself on factory farming and cruelty to animals, and I suddenly realized that what was on my plate were living things, with feelings. And I just couldn't disconnect myself from it any longer." **-Ellen DeGeneres**[2]

"I hold that the more helpless a creature, the more entitled it is to protection by man from the cruelty of man" **-Mohandas Gandhi**[8]

"I don't see why someone should lose their life just so you can have a snack."
-Russell Brand[2]

"I'm a vegan. I respect the environment, and I do my best to spread the importance of such an issue." **-Jared Leto**[2]

"The problem is that humans have victimized animals to such a degree that they are not even considered victims. They are not even considered at all. They are nothing; they don't count; they don't matter. They are commodities like TV sets and cell phones. We have actually turned animals into inanimate objects—sandwiches and shoes." **-Gary Yourofsky**[2]

"If a kid ever realized what was involved in factory farming, they would never touch meat again."
-James Cromwell[2]

"We all love animals. Why do we call some 'pets' and others 'dinner?'"
-K.D. Lang[2]

"Everyone has to find what is right for them, and it is different for everyone. Eating for me is how you proclaim your beliefs three times a day. That is why all religions have rules about eating. Three times a day, I remind myself that I value life and do not want to cause pain to or kill other living beings. That is why I eat the way I do." **-Natalie Portman**[1]

"I can't think of anything better in the world to be but a vegan."
-Alicia Silverstone[1]

"When I see bacon, I see a pig, I see a little friend, and that's why I can't eat it. Simple as that." **-Paul McCartney**[2]

"Non-violence leads to the highest ethics, which is the goal of all evolution. Until we stop harming all other living beings, we are still savages"
-Thomas Edison[2]

"I love animals. All animals. I wouldn't hurt a cat or a dog — or a chicken, or a cow. And I wouldn't ask someone else to hurt them for me."
-Peter Dinklage[2]

"If slaughterhouses had glass walls, we'd all be vegetarian."
-Paul McCartney[2]

"If you don't like seeing pictures of violence towards animals being posted, you need to help stop the violence, not the pictures." -Johnny Depp[2]

"The time will come when men such as I will look upon the murder of animals as they now look upon the murder of men." -Leonardo Da Vinci[2]

"People are the only animals that drink the milk of the mother of another species. All other animals stop drinking milk altogether after weaning. It is unnatural for a dog to nurse from a mother giraffe; it is just as unnatural for a human being to drink the milk of a cow." -Dr. Michael Klaper[2]

"If you don't want to be beaten, imprisoned, mutilated, killed or tortured then you shouldn't condone such behaviour towards anyone, be they human or not." -Moby[1]

"We choose to eat meat and have therefore built slaughterhouses for the animals and hospitals for us."-Akbarali Jetha[2]

"The question is not, Can they reason? Nor, Can they talk? but, Can they suffer?" -Jeremy Bentham[2]

"Animals don't have a voice, but I do. A loud one. A big fucking mouth. My voice is for them. And I'll never shut up while they suffer." -Ricky Gervais[2]

"You have just dined, and however scrupulously the slaughterhouse is concealed in the graceful distance of miles, there is complicity." -Ralph Waldo Emerson[3]

"The beef industry has contributed to more American deaths than all the wars of this century, all natural disasters, and all automobile accidents combined. If beef is your idea of "real food for real people" you'd better live real close to a real good hospital." **-Neal D. Barnard**[8]

"The most ethical diet just so happens to be the most environmentally sound diet and just so happens to be the healthiest." **-Dr. Michael Greger**[8]

"I've found that a person does not need protein from meat to be a successful athlete. In fact, my best year of track competition was the first year I ate a vegan diet." **-Carl Lewis**[8]

"It's not a requirement to eat animals, we just choose to do it, so it becomes a moral choice and one that is having a huge impact on the planet, using up resources and destroying the biosphere." **-James Cameron** [8]

If you could see or feel the suffering, you wouldn't think twice. Give back life. Don't eat meat. **-Kim Basinger** [8]

"There is no fundamental difference between man and animals in their ability to feel pleasure and pain, happiness, and misery." **-Charles Darwin**[2]

"One farmer says to me, 'You cannot live on vegetable food solely, for it furnishes nothing to make the bones with;' and so he religiously devotes a part of his day to supplying himself with the raw material of bones; walking all the while he talks behind his oxen, which, with vegetable-made bones, jerk him and his lumbering plow along in spite of every obstacle." **-Henry David Thoreau**[4]

"Behind every beautiful fur coat, there is a story. It is a bloody, barbaric story." **-Mary Tyler Moore**[2]

"No member of the animal kingdom ever did a thing to me. It's why I don't eat red meat or white fish. Don't give me no blue cheese. We're all members of the animal kingdom. Leave your brothers and sisters in the sea."
-**Prince**[8]

"Less meat, less heat, more life." -**Arnold Schwarzenegger**[10]

APPENDIX C
NEW VEGAN SUPPORT

Here is a short list of quick resources you can give to those who might be interested in going vegan. Take a picture, copy it, rip out the page—they are all loaded with information and resources.

1. **Challenge 22** – 22-day vegan challenge with support from mentors and dietitians. *https://www.challenge22.com/*
2. **Nutrition Facts** – is a strictly non-commercial, science-based public service provided by Dr. Michael Greger, providing free updates on the latest in nutrition research via bite-sized videos. *https://nutrition-facts.org/*
3. **The Vegan Society** – Founded in 1944 The Vegan Society has a wealth of information and resources available. *https://www.vegansociety.com/*
4. **Happy Cow** – An App and website. Happy Cow has an entire directory of Vegan, Vegetarian and plant-friendly restaurants, as well as resources on their website. *https://www.happycow.net/*
5. **Dr. Michael Klaper** – A talented teacher, known for explaining complex medical topics in plain English, Dr. Klaper invites you to take your health (wherever it may be at this moment) to the next level by enjoying and learning from his News Bites, DVDs, Videos On Demand, and Free Videos featured here at *https://www.DoctorKlaper.com*
6. **Physicians Committee for Responsible Medicine** – The Physi-

cians Committee is leading a revolution in medicine—putting a new focus on health and compassion. The Physicians Committee combines the clout and expertise of more than 12,000 physicians with the dedicated actions of more than 175,000 members across the United States and around the world. *https://www.pcrm.org/*

7. **Minimalist Baker** – Plant-based recipes requiring 10 ingredients or less, 1 bowl, or 30 minutes or less to prepare. *https://minimalist-baker.com/*

8. **Vegan Bodybuilding & Fitness** – Massive online resource for bodybuilding and athletes of all types, created by two-time natural bodybuilding champion Robert Cheeke. *http://veganbodybuilding.com*

9. **Dr. Fuhrman** – Dr. Joel Fuhrman's website has a variety of resources including 20-Day Transformation Programs. *https://www.drfuhrman.com/*

10. **Forks Over Knives** – Based on the groundbreaking documentary the FoK website has a meal planner and cooking course, as well as articles and recipes. *https://www.forksoverknives.com*

11. **No Meat Athlete** – Created by Matt Frazier No Meat Athlete is about giving you tools, not preaching. They are all about training tips, recipes, advice on how to transition, and the occasional dose of inspiration. *https://www.nomeatathlete.com*

12. **People for the Ethical Treatment of Animals** – PETA is the largest animal rights organization in the world, with more than 6.5 million members and supporters. Their site is filled with resources, current animal rights campaigns and free materials. *https://www.peta.org/*

REFERENCES

Chapter 1

1. Harvard Health Publishing. "The Right Plant-based Diet for You." Harvard Health. January, 2018. Accessed March 24, 2018. *https://www.health.harvard.edu/heart-health/ halt-heart-disease-with-a-plant-based-oil-free-diet-.*
2. "Why Most People Go Vegan." Vomadlife.com. December 16, 2016. *Accessed August 22, 2018. https://vomadlife.com/blogs/news/ why-most-people-go-vegan-2016-survey-results-reveal-all.*

Chapter 2

1. "Q&A on the carcinogenicity of the consumption of red meat and processed meat." WHO. October, 2015. Accessed March 14, 2018. http://www.who.int/features/qa/cancer-red-meat/en/.
2. Nyhan, Brendan and Jason Reifler. "When Corrections Fail: The persistence of political misperceptions." University of Michigan. *Accessed March 30, 2018. http://www.dartmouth.edu/~nyhan/ nyhan-reifler.pdf.*
3. Capps, Ashley. "You Probably Already Agree With All These Reasons to Go Vegan. I Did." Free From Harm. February 28, 2014. Accessed March 21, 2018. *https://freefromharm.org/why-vegan.*
4. "Why Most People Go Vegan." Vomadlife.com. December 16, 2016. *Accessed August 22, 2018. https://vomadlife.com/blogs/news/ why-most-people-go-vegan-2016-survey-results-reveal-all.*
5. Beam, Christopher. "Code Black." Slate.com. *January 11, 2010.*

Accessed August 12, 2018. http://www.slate.com/articles/news_and_politics/politics/2010/01/code_black.html.

6. Centorrino S, Djemai EB, Hopfensitz AC, and et al. "Honest signaling in trust interactions: smiles rated as genuine induce trust and signal higher earning opportunities." Evolution and Human Behavior. *January, 2015. Accessed March 30, 2018. https://www.sciencedirect.com/science/article/pii/S1090513814001007.*

Chapter 3

1. Yourofsky, Gary. "Dealing with Non-vegan Friends and Family." Bitesizevegan.com. October 27, 2014. Accessed October 26, 2018. *https://www.youtube.com/watch?v=76CbrC37hRk.*

2. "Why the Global Rise in Vegan and Plant-Based Eating Isn't A Fad." Foodrevolution.org. January 18, 2018. Accessed August 20, 2018. *https://foodrevolution.org/blog/vegan-statistics-global/.*

3. "Why Most People Go Vegan." Vomadlife.com. December 16, 2016. *Accessed August 22, 2018. https://vomadlife.com/blogs/news/why-most-people-go-vegan-2016-survey-results-reveal-all.*

4. Hyner, Christopher. "A Leading Cause of Everything: One Industry That Is Destroying Our Planet and Our Ability to Thrive on It." Georgetown Environmental Law Review. October 23, 2015.

5. Bellantonio, Marisa, et al. "The Ultimate Mystery Meat: Exposing the Secrets Behind Burger King and Global Meat Production." *Accessed June 20, 2018. http://www.mightyearth.org/mysterymeat/.*

6. "Facts." Cowspiracy.com. *Accessed 30 March, 2018. http://www.cowspiracy.com/facts/.*

7. Harvard Health Publishing. "The Right Plant-based Diet for You." Harvard Health. January, 2018. Accessed March 24, 2018. *https://www.health.harvard.edu/heart-health/halt-heart-disease-with-a-plant-based-oil-free-diet-.*

8. Feinberg, Matthew, Robb Willer and Chloe Kovacheff. "Extreme Protest Tactics Reduce Popular Support for Social Movements." Rotman School of Management, Working Paper No. 2911177. February 3, 2017. *Accessed 30 March, 2018. https://ssrn.com/abstract=2911177.*

Chapter 4

1. *Rodio, Michael. "The Vegan Diet of American Olympic Weight-lifter Kendrick Farris." MensJournal.com. June, 2016. Accessed August 12, 2018. https://www.mensjournal.com/food-drink/vegan-diet-american-olympic-weightlifter-kendrick-farris.*

2. Campell, Colin T. and Thomas M. Campbell II. *The China Study.* 2nd ed. Dallas, TX: BenBella Books, 2016.

3. Blahd, William. "High-Protein, Low-Carb Diets Explained." WebMD.com. 10 May, 2017. Accessed August 22, 2018. https://www.webmd.com/diet/guide/high-protein-low-carbohydrate-diets.

4. Natural Resources Conservation Service. "Balancing your Animals you're your Forage." USDA.gov. January, 2009. Accessed August 22, 2018. https://www.nrcs.usda.gov/Internet/FSE_DOCUMENTS/stelprdb1097070.pdf.

5. Pratt, Sean. "World's farmland total bigger than expected." Producer.com. November 30, 2017. Accessed August 24, 2018. https://www.producer.com/2017/11/worlds-farmland-total-bigger-expected/.

6. Tonstad S, Butler T, Yan R, Fraser GE. Type of Vegetarian Diet, Body Weight, and Prevalence of Type 2 Diabetes. Diabetes Care. May, 2009; 32(5): 791–796.

7. *"U.S. Poverty Statistics." FederalSafteyNet.com. Accessed October 12, 2018. http://federalsafetynet.com/us-poverty-statistics.html.*

8. "Update: A Report from the American Heart Association Statistics Committee and Stroke Statistics Subcommittee." Heart Disease and Stroke Statistics. Circulation 2008.

9. "Hispanic Health: Preventing Type 2 Diabetes." Centers for Disease Control and Prevention. September 18, 2017. Accessed October 21, 2018. https://www.cdc.gov/features/hispanichealth/index.html.

10. "Meat Contamination." PETA. 2010. Accessed March 24, 2018. https://www.peta.org/living/food/meat-contamination/.

11. *Remesar X, et al. "Estrogen in food: a factor influencing the development of obesity?" Eur J Nutr.* October, 1999; 38(5):247-53.

12. Harvard Health Publishing. "The Right Plant-based Diet for You." Harvard Health. January, 2018. Accessed March

24, 2018. *https://www.health.harvard.edu/heart-health/
halt-heart-disease-with-a-plant-based-oil-free-diet-*.

13. "Healthy Living." American Heart Association. Assessed October,
26 2018. https://www.heart.org/en/healthy-living/healthy-eating/
add-color.

14. "Diabetes Superfoods." American Diabetes Association. October
11, 2017. Accessed August 30, 2018. http://www.diabetes.org/
food-and-fitness/food/what-can-i-eat/making-healthy-food-choices/
diabetes-superfoods.html.

15. "Bon Jovi - Livin' On A Prayer Lyrics." MetroLyrics.com. Accessed
October 28, 2018. http://www.metrolyrics.com/livin-on-a-prayer-
lyrics-bon-jovi.html.

Chapter 5

1. Dwyer, Marge. "Millions may face protein deficiency as a result of human-caused carbon dioxide
emissions." Harvard University. *August 2, 2017. Accessed May
11, 2018. https://www.hsph.harvard.edu/news/press-releases/
climate-change-carbon-emissions-protein-deficiency/.*

2. *Van Allen, Jennifer. "Protein: Why it's so popular right now." The
Washington Post. July 22, 2014. Accessed May 11, 2018. https://
www.washingtonpost.com/lifestyle/wellness/protein-the-nutrient-du-
jour/2014/07/22/6a11b882-0b7b-11e4-b8e5-d0de80767fc2_story.
html?utm_term=.61a0f4034657.*

3. Messina M, and Barnes S. "The role of soy products in reducing risk
of cancer." *J Natl Cancer Inst.* 1991; 83:541-546.

4. Malekinejad H and Rezabakhsh A. Hormones in Dairy Foods and
Their Impact on Public Health - A Narrative Review Article. *Iran J
Public Health.* 2015 Jun; 44(6): 742–758.

5. Seema, Jayachandran and Rohini Pande. "Why Are Indian Children
Shorter Than African Children?" Harvard University. July 27, 2013.
Accessed June 23, 2018. http://scholar.harvard.edu/files/rpande/
files/why_are_indian_children_shorter_than_african_children.pdf.

6. Fergusson, Pamela. "Study with Dairy Ties Connects Vegan Milk

to Stunted Growth." Veg News. June 11, 2017. Accessed June 23, 2018. http://vegnews.com/articles/page.do?pageId=9640&catId=1.

7. Caspero, Alex. "3 Myths About Soy That You Should Stop Believing Right Now." *February 15, 2018. Accessed June 24, 2018. https://www.womenshealthmag.com/food/a17151261/is-soy-bad-for-you/.*

8. McCullough, Marji. "The Bottom Line on Soy and Breast Cancer Risk." Cancer.org. *August 2, 2012. Accessed June 26, 2018. http://blogs.cancer.org/expertvoices/2012/08/02/the-bottom-line-on-soy-and-breast-cancer-risk/.*

9. Messina M, Redmond G. "Effects of soy protein and soybean isoflavones on thyroid function in healthy adults and hypothyroid patients: a review of the relevant literature." *Thyroid.* March, 2006; 16(3):249-58.

10. *Fenton, Siobhan. "Vegans live longer than those who eat meat or eggs, research finds." August 2, 2016. Accessed August 13, 2018. https://www.independent.co.uk/life-style/health-and-families/health-news/vegan-meat-life-expectancy-eggs-dairy-research-a7168036.html.*

11. Brodwin, Erin. "The $37 billion supplement industry is barely regulated — and it's allowing dangerous products to slip through the cracks." Business Insider. *November 8, 2017. Accessed July 30, 2018. http://www.businessinsider.com/supplements-vitamins-bad-or-good-health-2017-8.*

12. Allen, Lindsay. "How common is vitamin B-12 deficiency?" American Society for Nutrition. *2009. Accessed July 30, 2018. https://pubag.nal.usda.gov/pubag/downloadPDF.xhtml?id=27177&content=PDF.*

13. "Artificial Insemination: What About the Other Animals?" Freakonomics.com. *November 22, 2011. Accessed August 1, 2018. http://freakonomics.com/2011/11/22/artificial-insemination-what-about-the-other-animals/.*

14. *Spencer EA, Appleby PN, Davey GK, Key TJ. "Diet and body mass index in 38000 EPIC-Oxford meat-eaters, fish-eaters, vegetarians and vegans." Int J Obes Relat Metab Disord. June, 2003; 27(6):728-34.*

15. *"Bigger Brains: Complex Brains for a Complex World." Smithsonian*

Institution. September 14, 2018. Accessed September 16, 2018. http:// humanorigins.si.edu/human-characteristics/brains.

16. *McDougall, John. "Extreme Nutrition: The Diet of Eskimos." April, 2015. Accessed September 17, 2018. https://www.drmcdougall.com/ misc/2015nl/apr/eskimos.htm.*

17. *"Largest mouth - terrestrial animal." GuinnessWorldRecords.com. Accessed October 28, 2108. http://www.guinnessworldrecords.com/ world-records/78607-largest-mouth-terrestrial-animal.*

18. Alena. "14 Reasons Why You Should Go Vegan in 2018." Nutri-ciously.com. *January 16, 2018. Accessed March 24, 2018. https:// nutriciously.com/why-go-vegan/.*

19. *Gambino, Megan. "What Was on the Menu at the First Thanksgiving?" November 21, 2011. Accessed September 30, 2018. https://www.smithsonianmag.com/history/ what-was-on-the-menu-at-the-first-thanksgiving-511554/.*

Chapter 6

1. Reign. Email to author. November 6, 2018.
2. Andrie D. Email to author. October 3, 2018.
3. Maayan P. Conversation with author. October 11, 2018.
4. Nichelle B. Email to author. October 3, 2018
5. Joshua H. Email to author. October 3, 2018.
6. Cynthia R. Email to author. October 14, 2018.
7. Nathan B. Email to author. September 27, 2018.
8. Eugenie G. Email to author. October 9, 2018.
9. Raluca C. Email to author. October 14, 2018.
10. Heather S. Email to author. October 11, 2018.
11. Jessica G. Email to author, October 12, 2018.
12. Elena I. Email to author. October 15, 2018.
13. Karen R. Email to author. October 19, 2018.

Appendix A

1. Holt-Giménez, E, Shattuck A, Altieri M, Herren H, Gliessman S. "We Already Grow Enough Food for 10 Billion People… and Still Can't End Hunger." *J Sustainable Agr*, May, 2012; 36. 595-98.
2. Capps, Ashley. "You Probably Already Agree With All These Rea-

sons to Go Vegan. I Did." Free From Harm. February 28, 2014. Accessed March 21, 2018. *https://freefromharm.org/why-vegan.*

3. "Wildlife Disserve: The USDA Wildlife Services' Inefficient and Inhumane Wildlife Damage Management Program." The Humane Society of the United States. *2015. Accessed June 24, 2018. http://www.humanesociety.org/assets/pdfs/wildlife/wildlife-services-white-paper-2015.pdf.*

4. Harvard Health Publishing. "The Right Plant-based Diet for You." Harvard Health. January, 2018. Accessed March 24, 2018. *https://www.health.harvard.edu/heart-health/halt-heart-disease-with-a-plant-based-oil-free-diet-*

5. Alena. "14 Reasons Why You Should Go Vegan in 2018." Nutriciously.com. *January 16, 2018. Accessed March 24, 2018. https://nutriciously.com/why-go-vegan/.*

6. "Meat Contamination." PETA. 2010. Accessed March 24, 2018. https://www.peta.org/living/food/meat-contamination/.

7. Hyner, Christopher. "A Leading Cause of Everything: One Industry That Is Destroying Our Planet and Our Ability to Thrive on It." Georgetown Environmental Law Review. October 23, 2015.

8. "11 Facts About Vegan Living." Do Something.org. *Accessed March 30, 2018. https://www.dosomething.org/facts/11-facts-about-vegan-living.*

9. "Statistics." The Vegan Society. *Accessed March 30, 2018. https://www.vegansociety.com/news/media/statistics*

10. Lusk JL, Norwood FB, Prickett RW. "Consumer Preferences for Farm Animal Welfare: Results of a Nationwide Telephone Survey." Department of Agricultural Economics Oklahoma State University. August 17, 2007. Accessed 3 June, 2018. http://cratefreefuture.com/pdf/American%20Farm%20Bureau-Funded%20Poll.pdf.

11. "17 Chicken Facts the Industry Doesn't Want You to Know." FreeFromHarm.org. *August 28, 2014. Accessed June 3, 2018. https://freefromharm.org/animalagriculture/chicken-facts-industry-doesnt-want-know/.*

12. Lehnardt, Karin. "56 Fresh Facts about Vegetarianism." *August*

19, 2016. *Accessed April 2, 2018. https://www.factretriever.com/ vegetarian-facts.*

13. "Lifespan." NutritionFacts.org. *Accessed April 2, 2018. https://nutritionfacts.org/topics/lifespan/.*

14. "Diabetes." NutritionFacts.org. *Accessed April 2, 2018. https://nutritionfacts.org/topics/diabetes/.*

15. Carney, Linda. "97% of People are Deficient in this Nutrient." *June 7, 2014. Accessed April 2, 2018. https://www.drcarney.com/blog/entry/97-of-people-are-deficient-in-this-nutrient.*

16. Eubanks, William. "30 Interesting Facts About Vegetarianism that Will Surprise You." GreenandGrowinig.org. *September 25, 2017. Accessed April 3, 2018. https://www.greenandgrowing.org/facts-about-vegetarianism/.*

17. Hackett, Jolinda. "Is Cheese Vegetarian?" TheSpruceEats.com. *https://www.thespruce.com/is-cheese-vegetarian-3378471. February 26, 2018. Accessed April 3, 2018.*

18. "What is Lactose Intolerance?" PCRM. *Accessed April 3, 2018.* www.pcrm.org/health/diets/vegdiets/what-is-lactose-intolerance

19. Bosch AC, O'Neill B, Sigge GO, Kerwath SE, Hoffman LC. "Heavy Metals in Marine Fish Meat and Consumer Health: a review." *J Sci Food Agric.* January, 2016; 96(1):32-48

20. "Benefits of Artificial insemination in Livestock." AnimalSmart.org. *Accessed April 3, 2018. http://animalsmart.org/animal-science/the-fields-of-animal-science/breeding-and-genetics/learn-more-about-artificial-insemination.*

21. *"Chicken Facts the Industry Doesn't Want You to Know." FreeFromHarm.org. August 28, 2014. Accessed April 3, 2018. https://freefromharm.org/animalagriculture/chicken-facts-industry-doesnt-want-know/.*

22. Bellantonio, Marisa, et al. "The Ultimate Mystery Meat: Exposing the Secrets Behind Burger King and Global Meat Production." *Accessed June 20, 2018. http://www.mightyearth.org/mysterymeat/. 32*

23. "Vegan Diets: Healthy and Humane." PETA. *Accessed April 3, 2018. https://www.peta.org/issues/animals-used-for-food/animals-used-food-factsheets/vegan-diets-healthy-humane/.*

24. Sharp, Ash." 60 Benefits of Going Vegan That Will Change Your Life." *Accessed April 3, 2018. https://www.veganmotivation. com/60-benefits-of-going-vegan/.*

25. "Some Vegan Facts." *Accessed April 3, 2018. http://www.somevegan-facts.com/.*

26. Spencer EA, Appleby PN, Davey GK, Key TJ. "Diet and body mass index in 38000 EPIC-Oxford meat-eaters, fish-eaters, vegetarians and vegans." *Int J Obes Relat Metab Disord.* June, 2003; 27(6):728-34.

27. Vegan Health. "Don't Feed Cancer." Viva! Health. *Accessed April 4, 2018. https://www.vivahealth.org.uk/veganhealth/dont-feed-cancer.*

28. Maruyama K, Oshima T, Ohyama K. "Exposure to exogenous estrogen through intake of commercial milk produced from pregnant cows." *Pediatr Int. February, 2010; 52(1):33-8*

29. Flanders, Timothy F, RN, CNP, PHD, et al. "A Review of Antibiotic Use in Food Animals: Perspective, Policy, and Potential." *Public Health Reports.* January-February, 2012; 127 (1): 4-22

30. "Facts." What the Health. *Accessed April 4, 2018. http://www.what-thehealthfilm.com/facts/.*

31. McVeigh, Karen. "Vegetarians less likely to develop cancer than meat eaters, says study." *June 30, 2009. Accessed April 4, 2018. https://www.theguardian.com/science/2009/jul/01/vegetarians-blood-cancer-diet-risk.*

32. "11 Facts About Vegan Living." Do Something.org. *Accessed April 4, 2018. https://www.dosomething.org/facts/11-facts-about-vegan-living.*

33. Jacobson, Michael. "Six Arguments For a Greener Diet: How a More Plant-based Diet Could Save Your Health and the Environment." Washington, DC: Center for Science in the Public Interest, 2006.

34. Thornton, Phillip, et al. "Livestock and climate change." Livestock exchange. International Livestock Research Institute. November, 2011.

35. "The Facts." Cowspiracy. *Accessed April 7, 2018.* http://www.cow-spiracy.com/facts/.

36. Zielinski, Sarah. "Ocean Dead Zones Are Getting Worse Globally

Due to Climate Change." Smithsonian.com. November 10, 2014. Accessed April 7, 2018.

37. Mood A, Brooke P. "Estimating the Number of Fish Caught in Global Fishing Each Year." July, 2010. Accessed April 7, 2018. http://fishcount.org.uk/published/std/fishcountstudy.pdf.

38. Sansoucy, R. "Livestock - a driving force for food security and sustainable development." FAO. Accessed April 7, 2018. http://www.fao.org/docrep/v8180t/v8180t07.htm.

39. Oppenlander, Richard A. *Less Meat, and Taking Baby Steps Won't Work*. Minneapolis, MN: Langdon Street, 2013.

40. *"The carbon foodprint of five diets compared." ShrinkThatFootprint.com. Accessed April 7, 2018. http://shrinkthatfootprint.com/food-carbon-footprint-diet.*

41. "A Vegan Diet Can Help With Impotence." PETA. *2010. Accessed April 7, 2018. https://www.peta.org/living/food/impotence/?search=impotence.*

42. Gale CR, Deary IJ, Schoon I, Batty GD. "IQ in childhood and vegetarianism in adulthood: 1970 British cohort study." *BMJ*. February, 2007; 334(7587):245.

43. Hänninen O, Rauma AL, Kaartinen K, Nenonen M. "Vegan diet in physiological health promotion." *Acta Physiol Hung. 1999; 86(3-4):171-80.*

44. Schagen SK, Zampeli VA, Makrantonaki E, Zouboulis CC. "Discovering the link between nutrition and skin aging." *Dermatoendocrinol*. July, 2012; 4(3): 298–307.

45. Food & Drink. "9 Facts About Factory Farming That Will Break Your Heart." Huffington Post. *March 17, 2014. Accessed April 7, 2018. https://www.huffingtonpost.com/2014/03/17/factory-farming-facts_n_4063892.html.*

46. Ketler, Alanna. "10 Alarming Facts About Factory Farms That Will Break Your Heart." CollectiveEvolution.com. *March 21, 2014. Accessed April 7, 2018. http://www.collective-evolution.com/2014/03/21/10-alarming-facts-about-factory-farms-that-will-break-your-heart/.*

Appendix B

1. "13 Inspiring Celebrity Quotes on Why Veganism is the Bomb." MercyforAnimals.org. Accessed October 28, 2018. *https://mercyfor-animals.org/13-inspiring-celebrity-quotes-on-why-veganism.*

2. "112 Inspiring & Truthful Vegan Quotes." TheFriendlyFig.com. Accessed October 28, 2018. *https://thefriendlyfig.com/2015/02/19/inspirational-vegan-quotes/.*

3. "Veganism Quotes." Goodreads.com. Accessed October 28, 2018. *https://www.goodreads.com/quotes/tag/veganism.*

4. Jeff. "Vegan Quotes – Socrates, Buddha, Einstein and Others on Going Vegan." ChangeforaYear.com. February 19, 2013. Accessed October 28, 2018. *http://www.changeforayear.com/2013/02/19/socrates-buddha-einstein-and-others-on-going-vegan/.*

5. "Vegetarian Scholars & Inventors." ProCon.org. January 11, 2012. Accessed October 28, 2018. *https://vegetarian.procon.org/view.resource.php?resourceID=004602.*

6. Tesla, Nikola. "The Problem of Increasing Human Energy." PBS. Accessed October 28, 2018. *https://www.pbs.org/tesla/res/res_art09.html.*

7. "I had no Idea They're Vegan." Breesharp.com. Accessed October 28, 2018. *http://www.breesharp.com/famous-vegetarians—quotes.html.*

8. "100 (More) Inspiring Vegan Quotes." TheFriendlyFig.com. Accessed October 28, 2018. *https://thefriendlyfig.com/2018/05/10/100-more-vegan-quotes/.*

9. Aspey, James. "Vow of Silence for the Animals" Speech, Holistic Holliday At Sea, February 24.

10. Arnold Schwarzenegger. "Less Meat Less Heat." Commercial, November 17, 2016. Accessed October 28, 2018. *https://www.youtube.com/watch?v=c3q-7ish6vk.*

17968186R00113

Printed in Great Britain
by Amazon